From the Cold War
to the War on Terror

From the Cold War to the War on Terror

The Personal Story of an RAF Armourer and Engineer from Nuclear Weapons to Bomb Disposal

Mick Haygarth

FRONTLINE BOOKS

First published in Great Britain in 2019 by
Frontline Books
An imprint of
Pen & Sword Books Ltd
Yorkshire – Philadelphia

ISBN 978 1 52675 934 4

Printed and bound in the UK by TJ International Ltd,
Padstow, Cornwall.

Pen & Sword Books Limited incorporates the imprints of Atlas,
Archaeology, Aviation, Discovery, Family History, Fiction, History,
Maritime, Military, Military Classics, Politics, Select, Transport,
True Crime, Air World, Frontline Publishing, Leo Cooper, Remember
When, Seaforth Publishing, The Praetorian Press, Wharncliffe
Local History, Wharncliffe Transport, Wharncliffe True Crime
and White Owl.

For a complete list of Pen & Sword titles please contact

PEN & SWORD BOOKS LIMITED
47 Church Street, Barnsley, South Yorkshire, S70 2AS, England
E-mail: enquiries@pen-and-sword.co.uk
Website: www.pen-and-sword.co.uk

Or

PEN AND SWORD BOOKS
1950 Lawrence Rd, Havertown, PA 19083, USA
E-mail: Uspen-and-sword@casematepublishers.com
Website: www.penandswordbooks.com

Contents

Introduction

Squadron Leader Mick Haygarth RAF (Retired) had a full and distinguished thirty-eight-year career in the Royal Air Force as a Weapons Technician and Engineering Officer. During that time, he visited thirty-four countries in the line of duty and worked closely with the Royal Navy, the Army and numerous other nations. He carried out operational tours of duty in Italy, the Falkland Islands, Kosovo, Iraq and the UAE. This book is a personal account of his experiences written from the perspective of a weapons tradesman and Aircraft Engineering Officer who went on to become one of the RAF's senior bomb disposal specialists.

He left home a few weeks before his 17th birthday to join the Royal Air Force as a weapons technician. At the time, everything seemed very normal and routine but his thirty-eight-year career turned out to be anything but. From training with other nations all over the world; fast roping out of helicopters with US Army Rangers; being driven around Basrah in the back of a beaten up taxi wearing civilian clothes with a 9mm pistol stuck in his waistband, to convoying at speed around Baghdad with the United States Army looking for unexploded bombs.

All of these events were extraordinary and way out of the comfort zone for an RAF engineer.

Acknowledgements

I never kept a diary throughout my career; therefore, this book has been written entirely from memory and the exact dates, times and places are as close as possible to what I recall.

If you recognise yourself in the book, either good or bad, just be proud that you made it and that you made a lasting impression on me.

There are too many people to mention individually who have crossed my path over my thirty-eight years in the RAF. I would like to thank you all for your friendship, guidance and professionalism.

A big thank you to my family who have supported me throughout my career. To my parents, who were my taxi and laundry service prior to me getting married. To my wife and kids, who have had to put up with me working crazy hours and who have held everything together without complaint as I visited the thirty-four countries that I have been so fortunate to see. The trips ranged from a couple of days to six months and several years away from home doing weekly commuting from postings in the UK. Not once did anyone say that they did not want me to go. (Well OK, maybe a couple of times but only for the postings that I had no choice over.)

Chapter 1

Swinderby and Halton

I don't remember a great deal about the early years of my RAF career and to be honest I'm not even sure what made me want to join in the first place. However, once I had set my mind to it I was determined to do whatever it took to enlist. I do remember going to the Armed Forces Careers Office (AFCO) and asking to join as an Airframes and Propulsion dual trade apprentice, more commonly known as a Rigger/Sooty Split Brain. I was told that there were no vacancies in that particular trade but I could be a Direct Entry (DE) Weapons Technician if that appealed to me. I did a bit of research and decided that rather than wait for an opening in my first choice of trade the weapon tech route was the one for me, especially as it was using the DE route.

I have often been asked if there was anything I would change about my career path and I have always said no and I honestly mean it. The weapons tech route has offered me the widest experience of work, opportunities to travel and has forged my career right through to my penultimate posting.

On 30 August 1977 my parents and my brother took me to Darlington Railway Station and saw me onto the train that would take me to Newark Northgate. I was met at Newark by a scary-looking corporal, who ushered me and the other arrivals onto the waiting bus that would take us to RAF Swinderby.

Decent accommodation in one of the new blocks meant that we had carpets and not linoleum floors, which would prove to make domestic evenings a lot easier as it meant vacuuming the carpets rather than polishing the floors.

Everybody started the process of unpacking and sorting out our bed spaces and rooms, and we were called forward during this process for the obligatory haircut. I knew this was going to happen and had had a haircut the previous week in preparation, and although I was quite happy to be shorn like a sheep I was a bit shocked when I was asked to pay for the privilege.

Basic training was everything you expected it to be with lots of physical training (PT), drill practice, classroom work on the history and ethos of the RAF, and RAF Regiment ground defence training. Towards the end of the six-week training course the culmination of all of the training elements were brought together with some camping and exercising in Sherwood Forest. Throughout the basic training phase, we didn't have a great deal of spare time but that was not much of a concern to me as at a few weeks short of my 17th birthday I was too young to drink and too young to drive so had nowhere to go and no way of getting there. I remember being allowed out into Lincoln for an afternoon in our number one uniform and a few of us had a few hours to go to the hospital at RAF Nocton Hall to visit one of our flight members who had collapsed during a cross-country run.

It would soon be time for our first pay day and in these times before everybody had a bank account we were introduced to the weekly pay parade. We had to wear our uniform including headdress and march to towards a table at which the issuing officer would be sat. We would salute, state our name and service number and on confirmation of our identity he would count out our pay amount, which we would sign for and march out of the room.

As part of our introduction to the RAF we were scheduled to travel to RAF Waddington for an air experience flight in a state-of-the-art VC10 aircraft. I was not to know it at the time but I would still be flying in VC10s some thirty years later. We arrived at RAF Waddington and as I climbed on board I was overflowing with a mixture of excitement and trepidation as this was the first time I had ever been on an aeroplane. The first thing I noticed was that the seats faced backwards and there was very little legroom for anybody who was taller than about 5ft 6in, but I settled into my seat and prepared for my first experience of flying.

As we thundered down the runway 'backwards' my excitement was building and soon we were airborne and flying around the skies above Lincolnshire. As the flight was only scheduled to last for forty minutes or so we stayed at a fairly low altitude, therefore making it a bit bumpier than normal, and soon I started to feel a bit worse for wear. The result of this was that, along with sampling my first flight in an aeroplane I also got to sample my first incident of air sickness and my first use of a sick bag, all rounded off with the indignity of carrying my first half full sick bag off an aeroplane to deposit in the bins with everybody watching on and trying hard to contain their laughter.

The RAF Regiment training was one of my first lasting memories with the much talked about trips to the respirator testing facility (gas chamber). Each of us would be required to remove our gas mask and recite our service number and then our favourite football team and then anything else that would ensure you got your first taste of CS gas (just to give you the confidence that your gas mask worked). I didn't know it at the time but the Regiment training would have many changes throughout my career but getting gassed and taking my respirator with me everywhere I went and not needing it would be two of the constants in my thirty-eight years of service.

Passing out parade came around quickly with family attending and the first of many 'proud moments' was soon assigned to history.

A few days' down time followed the passing out parade at Swinderby and then it was off to RAF Halton, again by train, for the start of my trade training. The start of a very long and difficult nine months of training on Aircraft Weapons Direct Entry Course Number 16, or AWD 16 as it was known.

Again, my recollection of this time is quite sketchy but the key memories revolve around the basic workshop phase (hacking and bashing), electrics, PT, learning all about proper armament stuff, education phase (maths and physics), and the whole of RAF Halton being a testing ground for the emerging punk rockers and the era of born-again Teddy Boys. The accommodation was a step back in time as the carpeted floors were replaced with linoleum and therefore no more vacuuming on domestic evenings but lots of floor polish and heavy floor buffers.

The weekly NAAFI bop was split down the middle with the emerging Johnny Rottens in one corner and the revived Elvis Presleys in the other. I had always been a fan of Elvis Presley and other rock 'n' roll legends so I naturally gravitated to that corner. I found a shop in a nearby town that sold all of the regalia associated with the 1950s and '60s and kitted myself out in black drainpipe trousers, black beetle-crushers and a red drape jacket trimmed in black velvet. Fortunately for me this was long before the days of portable cameras, not to mention smart phones, so it is highly unlikely that any incriminating images exist.

During my time at Halton it was the Queen's Silver Jubilee and I got my first taste of how the military often manned such auspicious occasions. As the longer-duration courses at Halton had more time to catch up on missed studies we were chosen to represent the RAF at the commemoration service at Westminster Abbey. We were bussed down to London early on the morning of the service, mingled around outside the Abbey for a while and were then shown to our seats inside in time for the Queen to arrive and for the service to take place. After proceedings were over we were held back until all the senior dignitaries had left and we were then taken back to Halton by bus. Early start, lots of hanging around and a late finish was the stock routine for rent-a-crowd.

Halton was also the scene of my first encounter with the Scottish race and their warped obsession with hating the English. I had never encountered such bigotry before and indeed I would come to experience far worse on my tours north of the border later in my career. As we were watching a replay of the Scottish football supporters trashing the Wembley pitch having beaten England, I was told that as English football supporters we were always living in the past and constantly digging up and falling back on our World Cup victory in 1966. The lecture might have held some weight if it hadn't been dished out by someone with 'Bannockburn 1314' tattooed on his arm! And he thought I was living in the past!

After a very long and intensive nine months of academic work, technical work and phase exams, the final exams came around, which I passed, and we would now prepare for the passing out parade and wait for notification of posting.

Passing out parade came and went along with promotion to the rank of Junior Technician (JT) and the mighty increase in pay that this brought.

Postings were in and the course graduates were to be sent to various different locations all over the country. I had really enjoyed the aircraft phases of the training and was hoping to go to somewhere with aircraft. The moment of truth was here ... RAF West Raynham.

Two questions sprung immediately to mind on hearing of my impending posting:

Where the hell is RAF West Raynham?
What on earth do they have there?

All would soon be revealed.

Chapter 2

West Raynham

A couple of weeks at home to recharge my batteries and then on the train again and off to RAF West Raynham. Not the easiest of journeys as you had to go down the country then across and I eventually arrived at King's Lynn to be met by the Station Motor Transport (MT) people with a bus to take me to my new unit. After driving into the back and beyond outer reaches of rural Norfolk we eventually arrived at the camp gates and I was met by one of the armament section corporals. Having spent the past year in training establishments I spoke subserviently to the corporal, who looked as pleased as punch when I called him 'corporal'. RAF West Raynham was the HQ for the Bloodhound missile force and I was informed that I would be working in the Explosive Fitment Bay (EFB) where routine daily task included fitting all explosive and aerodynamic components (wings and fins) to the missiles before they were taken out onto the launchers and vice versa as they came back in for maintenance. A fairly dull and mundane task but a fairly easy introduction to life in the RAF.

After a month or so at work I took some leave as my parents had managed to get me a driving test cancellation and I headed off home for some intensive driving lessons with my parents and then my test. On the day of my test I felt absolutely awful and nearly threw up when I did the emergency stop. I passed and then went to the doctors to be told that I had glandular fever and was signed off sick for a couple of weeks. This period of time off work gave me the opportunity to look for and buy a car and by the time I returned to West Raynham I was the proud owner of a Mark 1 Ford Escort.

Once back at work, and now with a driving licence, I decided I wanted to drive the huge Side Loading Fork Lift Truck (SLFLT) that was used to move the Bloodhound missiles around the unit and load and unload them from the launchers. First, I had to get a military driving licence, which in those days involved driving something big and getting a licence for everything smaller. This done, I started my SLFLT instruction and soon became qualified to drive the fork version, followed closely by the beam version. Despite having driven the SLFLT for several years at West Raynham, once the more stringent licensing came into force later in my career my qualification was deemed not to be transferrable and my qualification to drive forklift vehicles was withdrawn.

With this new-found skill came the opportunity to go on the RAF Germany missile resupply trips. Every week a small team would take three missiles to RAF Marham, load them onto a Hercules transport aircraft and fly with them to one of the three RAF Germany units that had Bloodhound detachments (Laarbruch, Wildenrath and Bruggen).

The unit personnel would unload and load the Hercules whilst we went duty free shopping in the NAAFI and then it was back onto the Hercules for the flight back to Marham, unload the missiles and drive back to West Raynham. This was a great opportunity to see other RAF units, get over my flying sickness and stock up my drinks cabinet.

However, it was during one of these resupply trips that disaster struck. As we unloaded one of the missiles from the aircraft loading trailer the forks dipped without input from me and the missile tumbled off the trailer, narrowly missing the Chief Tech in charge of the team and landing upside down on the aircraft pan at RAF Marham. So began an extremely stressful clear-up operation and on return to West Raynham it was announced that a unit enquiry would be instigated. As a still very green and wet behind the ears airman, I was guided through this process by the Chief Tech and after months of interviews and statements it was decided that we were partly to blame (still not sure how) and we were fined a nominal amount. Although my view that the ageing SLFLT was no longer fit for purpose was not shared by the enquiry president, brand spanking new replacement SLFLTs turned up shortly after.

For the superstitious amongst you the Bloodhound missile serial number was 3343, which adds up to 13.

After a year or so at West Raynham I was asked if I wanted to go on a four-week detachment to RAF Binbrook. Whilst I was enjoying my time at West Raynham, this detachment would give me the opportunity to see more of the RAF, to serve some time on a flying station (Lightning aircraft flew from Binbrook in those days) but more importantly it would reduce my weekly commute to and from Durham by about ninety minutes or so each way. I spent my time at Binbrook working in the Missile Servicing Flight (MSF) servicing Red Top and Firestreak missiles. It was during this detachment that I was introduced to more intense and longer-lasting station exercises, where my job was to sit in an old wooden box in the farthest corner of MSF with no weapon or lights and guard against intruders.

Having bought a Ford Escort, I spent the majority of my spare time in the motor club repairing and upkeeping my car in order to make the weekly journey back to Bishop Auckland, predominantly to see my girlfriend although I ended up spending quite a bit of time repairing the car to make the return journey. After a couple of years of doing this trip, Dawn and I decided to get married and we did so in 1980 and moved into married quarters close to West Raynham.

Throughout my tour at West Raynham I worked in all of the different armament sections including the Explosive Storage Area (ESA) and Small Arms Servicing Bay. I also got my first taste of Explosive Ordnance Disposal (EOD) as the driver for the EOD team. In those days EOD was carried out by an EOD Senior Non-Commissioned Officer (SNCO) in a Land Rover with a driver who drove round on routine exercises making things go bang with thunder flashes or detonators. This was fairly insignificant at the time but nevertheless was my first taste of EOD in what would be a career defined by that specialism.

One of the most memorable sights to behold whilst at RAF West Raynham was the regular Friday morning dance of the Bloodhound missiles. Every Friday without fail the radars would start turning and along with them in unison the missile launchers with the Bloodhound missiles on board would start tracking the paths identified by the radars. Then in the distance you would see the dark smoke trails of aircraft approaching the base as they weaved and sank to ridiculously low level to try and avoid the radars and ensure that they were not locked on to by them.

In an instant two or three Vulcan bombers came hurtling across the radar sites at altitudes of less than 100ft as if to say, 'Here we are but you can't lock on to us because we are too low.' Few sights if any can top the vision of low-flying Vulcan bombers but as I would soon find out the Buccaneers would provide just as good a spectacle, if not better on some occasions.

One if my most vivid memories of my time at West Raynham was when a newly promoted JT was posted in and although he settled very quickly into life there was something a bit weird about him. As the weeks went by he seemed to become more distant and rarely went out with the boys but chose to lock himself away in his room, only emerging to go to work and occasionally go for a meal in the mess.

After a few months he went away on a week's leave but never returned to work on time and very soon after he was declared absent without leave (AWOL). About three weeks later a dishevelled-looking individual walked through the camp gates and reported to the guardroom, where he was recognised as the AWOL airman and arrested by the police. He was charged with being AWOL and, because of the amount of time he had been missing, his charge had to be heard by the Station Commander and I was given the dubious honour of being his escort. We were marched into the office of the Station Commander and halted a few feet away from his desk. The charge of being AWOL was read out and he was asked if he had anything to say. He said that he did have something to offer in his defence and went on to explain how he was at a Jehovah's Witness meeting at a small town in Germany and they had explained to him how bad it was for the military to do what they did and suggested that people should not join the military. He decided at this point that he agreed with their point of view and decided not to return to work. When asked why he had chosen to come back he pointed out that he had only done so to pick up his stuff and had been arrested. He was sentenced to fourteen days in the military prison in Colchester.

After his sentence he returned to work but was only permitted to carry out menial tasks in low-security, non-sensitive areas and always had to have an escort with him. This was very restrictive for the management team as most of the places we worked in were in high-security areas and losing another person just to babysit him was a drain on the manpower.

Very soon after, he disappeared again and this time he didn't return for a month or so. Once back he went through the same routine of arrest and charge and again I was selected to be his escort when he was marched into the Station Commander's office. This time he told the Station Commander that he had been beamed up by aliens and he had only returned when the aliens had released him. I found it really hard listening to this, standing to attention, and I was now struggling to contain my laughter as he described his out of this world experience. This time he was sentenced to twenty-eight days in Colchester and dismissed from the RAF.

As he was no longer coming back to work his belongings had to be packed up and put into storage, where they would be held until he returned to get them after his sentence was complete. One of the chief technicians was nominated to go to the individual's room to itemise and pack up his belongings and I was nominated as his assistant. As we entered the room there was a strange musty smell and the room was in total darkness as the windows had all been blacked out. We turned on the light to be met by a room full of rubbish, the bed had been dismantled and the mattress was on the floor with some very grubby sheets curled up on it. There were clothes and rubbish everywhere and ashtrays full of very suspicious-looking roll-your-own cigarettes. We packed everything into boxes and took it to a storage hangar, where it was locked away until he returned to collect it prior to leaving the RAF.

It was during this first tour of duty that I witnessed the standard leaving ritual for all armourers and in particular those that worked in explosive storage areas or the like. As well as going out for a few drinks it was 'the law' that on your final day at work you would be unceremoniously dumped into the static water tank. This was a large concrete pool with water in it that was used as a method of replenishing fire engines or for feeding water pumps in the event of a serious fire in the area. They were generally about 5ft deep and surrounded by a fence to stop people falling in them, but on these occasions the fence was just an obstacle to be cleared before you hit the water. I left in the summer so was fairly fortunate in that the water was a reasonable temperature and I was just held by my arms and legs and hurled over the fence. However, during my time there I had seen people dropped from the raised forks of a forklift truck and even seen people break the ice on the top of the tank as they entered the water. Looking back, many of these occasions would be construed as bullying or physical abuse in today's society but that was just how it was in those days.

Lots of people on the unit had really nice cars and it became apparent that the best, and probably the only, way for me to get something similar was to join the thousands of people who were serving in RAF Germany and buy a tax-free car. I filled in the application form and a few months later was told that I was to be posted to RAF Laarbruch to serve on 16 Squadron. This move onto the Buccaneer aircraft required me to attend a Buccaneer weapons course at RAF Honington, which I did and swiftly put my belongings into storage, packed my wife back to her parents and caught the ferry from Felixstowe to Zeebrugge.

Chapter 3

Laarbruch

My ageing Ford Escort made the journey to RAF Laarbruch without any problems but it soon became apparent that the car was not going to last much longer and it was extremely unlikely to pass the British Forces Germany (BFG) version of the MOT. That said, it was still going OK and I was hopeful that it would last a couple of months until I could get everything else sorted.

On arrival at Laarbruch I was told that 16 Squadron were on detachment in the USA and that I would be working in the station armoury until they returned. I was put into the small arms section, which also covered the Aircraft Servicing Flight (ASF) doing the more in-depth work on Buccaneer, Hunter and Jaguar aircraft. Again, a great experience and the ideal way for me to hone my newly acquired aircraft servicing skills. Once 16 Squadron returned from the USA, I was told that I would be staying in the armoury for a few additional months, but having spoken to friends on 16 Squadron they informed me that I was needed. I approached the armoury warrant officer (WO), who grudgingly agreed to let me go but insisted that I did another duty armourer duty before I left (thanks for that). Duty done, I bade goodbye to the armoury and joined 16 Squadron.

My car was now on its last legs so I ordered my tax-free Ford Escort XR3, which took a couple of months to arrive. Just about everybody in BFG had either an XR3 or an Audi Coupe and the art was to try and make yours stand out from the crowd. I did so by getting some huge go faster stripes applied to mine.

In the meantime, I was getting hassle from the RAF Police as my old car was sitting rotting in a car park outside one of the accommodation blocks and they wanted me to move it. One of the station firemen asked me if he could have the wheels off my old car and we made a deal in that he could have the wheels if he disposed of the car for me. It was gone the following day.

My time on 16 Squadron was fantastic, as indeed was life in general at Laarbruch. We worked a standard squadron shift system of alternating weeks between day and night shift. There were lots of station exercises in those heady Cold War days with getting called out in the early hours of the morning a routine occurrence as the fire engines drove around the married quarter patch with sirens blaring. Everybody rushed to work and started on the task of generating as many combat armed aircraft as possible. For the Buccaneer Force this task involved re-roling the aircraft into the required configuration and then fitting an assortment, or combination, of electronic countermeasure (ECM) pods, missiles, bombs, fuel tanks and laser designation pods.

Once all possible aircraft had been generated it was a case of sitting around until the other squadrons had achieved the task and then the exercise would be terminated. At that point, a large proportion of the station personnel would hand in their personal weapon and go home but for the flying squadrons all aircraft had to be re-roled in preparation for the routine flying programme and this meant that the armourers would always be the last to finish.

Monthly two- or three-day exercises were also routine with the scenario always beginning with conventional warfare and culminating in nuclear armageddon, where we would load up our aircraft with nuclear weapons, send them off to do their deed and then sit around in gas masks until the war was over. This phase often resulted in sitting around for up to twelve hours in full nuclear protection gear. If possible we would always try and lock ourselves into a personnel or equipment shelter, where we could take off our masks without being caught. Every knock on the shelter door meant trying to shout out in a muffled voice trying to pretend that we were still wearing our masks, followed by the manic rush to put them back on if it was somebody that we had to let in.

As part of the strategic nuclear deterrent it was routine to carry out load training with nuclear weapons on a monthly basis. It was on one of these occasions when the nuclear weapon safety evaluation team called a practice fire as we were carrying out the loading procedure. In the event of an emergency, the whole process was choreographed like a dance and everybody had their own specific job to do. Mine was to phone the emergency services and open the shelter doors, which I did in meticulous fashion as practised on numerous occasions. On opening the shelter doors, it was clear that all was not as routine as it should be. There were people running in every direction and vehicles with blue flashing lights appearing from every corner of the airfield. The Load Team Leader was shocked by the thoroughness of the overall station response and asked if I had told the emergency services that it was only a practice. I replied that I had read out the details verbatim from the loading manual and therefore had not mentioned practice. After everybody had calmed down it was good to see that the actions we had practised and the response from across the unit had worked as designed.

I had the opportunity to attend a parachuting course whilst at Laarbruch and travelled to the Rhine Army Parachute Centre at Sennelager. This was my first introduction to the Army and pretty much helped me form an opinion that would last throughout my career. The course was a great opportunity and very enjoyable but two specific incidents will be forever ingrained on my mind.

The first was when a rather large Army student changed his mind about jumping and he wedged himself in the aircraft door. After a few seconds of heated discussion, he carried out an assisted departure of the aircraft (pushed by the instructor), his static line parachute deployed and as he descended he clearly forgot all of the drills he had been taught. He hit the ground with an almighty thump, heels first and then head.

His parachute started dragging him across the landing zone and the Army supervisor just kept shouting at him on the loudspeaker system to get up and pull his chute in. After a minute or so I mentioned to the supervisor that I thought he might be hurt, but he told me to shut up and carried on shouting at the student. After another minute or so they sent a vehicle and instructor to help and on arrival it was clear he was suffering from concussion having suffered a heavy blow to his head. He went off to hospital and never returned to the course.

A few days later we were on our second jump of the day and as we exited the aircraft it was obvious that we were a long way from the drop zone. As we all tried our hardest to steer our chutes to glide to the right place it was clear that we weren't all going to make it. The guy I travelled with from Laarbruch ended up dangling on his parachute from a tree. I made a valiant attempt to make the drop zone but at the last minute realised that I was not going to clear the final row of trees, made a hard-right turn and smashed into the eighteenth fairway of the Rhine Army Golf Course. A sprung bone in my shoulder and a torn groin muscle equalled the end of my parachuting course.

Having passed my promotion exam whilst at West Raynham, I was soon promoted to corporal and was told that I would be going on the RAF Germany Corporals Course. This was held at RAF Gatow in Berlin and was an absolute eye-opener. Travel from West Germany to Berlin was by train through the Berlin corridor. Prior to entering East Germany, the train doors were chained from the inside and were not unchained until we crossed into West Berlin. This was still Cold War Europe and long before the Berlin wall came down. The course involved mainly classroom work with the highlight of the week being the bus trip into East Berlin wearing our RAF number one uniform.

Also during this tour came my first real detachment to RAF Decimomannu (Deci) in Sardinia. It was a regular detachment each year for the bombing squadrons and it presented the aircrew with the opportunity to drop live high-explosive bombs. It also gave the ground crew the opportunity to support these bombing events. For most of the trades this was not much different to their normal work but for the armourers it was a unique opportunity to load real bombs and not have to take them off again. The majority of the bombs functioned as designed but for the occasional ones that did not it then deteriorated into a blame game that normally boiled down to two possibilities: did the armourers fit them properly and connect all the right bits – YES. Did the aircrew select all the right switches – PROBABLY NOT.

The social side of the Deci detachments were real old school work hard, play hard rules. Many happy nights in the Nuralgi Club drinking into the early hours and singing songs before stumbling back to bed and then getting up ready to load more bombs.

The Deci wall was a unique work of art that was decorated by all visiting squadrons. Some of the artwork was outstanding whilst other pieces were basic but they all added to the fantastic piece of folklore that I managed to get my name and design onto on the two occasions that I was detached there.

I was also lucky enough to go on a detachment to Canada for Exercise Maple Flag. We started the trip with a weekend in Edmonton before flying to Canadian Air Force Base Cold Lake, which was in the middle of nowhere. We worked hard and played hard for three weeks and on our weekend off we made a road trip to the Canadian Rockies, taking in all of the tourist destinations between Calgary, Banff and Jasper. It was a route that I would repeat on holiday with Dawn many years later.

Towards the end of my tour the end of the Buccaneer aircraft in RAF Germany was also signalled with the introduction to service of the Tornado. The two Buccaneer squadrons joined into one and the number of aircraft were slowly reduced and returned to the UK to supplement the home squadrons, which were all moving to RAF Lossiemouth. As part of his own idea for celebrating this occasion, the Senior Engineering Officer (SEngO) asked for volunteers to paint one of the squadron aircraft completely black. We did the work over a weekend and the final result was stunning. However, the following week the aircraft was spotted on a flying sortie and the powers that be at RAF Germany HQ ordered it to be repainted in the standard camouflage colours. Needless to say, that was another weekend at work to put right the wrong.

This draw down meant that ASF had to be split into two distinct areas: one for Buccaneer and one for Tornado. The Tornado people turned up with a bit of a chip on their shoulder and started to put people's noses out of joint with their demands and attitude. Because of this the Buccaneer half of ASF had 'Not Tornado' badges made for their coveralls to distinguish them.

As a culmination to the Buccaneer draw down in Germany, the combined squadron was selected to attend Exercise Red Flag, which took place at Nellis Air Force Base in Nevada USA, just outside Las Vegas. There would only be two aircraft going, to carry out laser designation for the Jaguar squadrons dropping laser-guided bombs, and therefore the support team would only be very small. I was fortunate enough to be chosen as one of only two armourers supporting the detachment. We had a work-up phase at RAF Lossiemouth, during which almost everything that could go wrong went wrong, resulting in numerous role equipment removal and fits and numerous ejection seat problems as well. This proved to be a good, bad omen, as during the six-week America detachment not a single thing went wrong.

Las Vegas itself to a first-time visitor was mesmerising and several of us made it our mission to visit every single casino during our time there. Mission accomplished. We also took the opportunity to visit the Grand Canyon, Los Angeles and San Francisco.

The detachment was so small in size that it was fully self-sufficient. Both Buccaneer aircraft, support equipment, support personnel and the support Hercules travelled as a package all the way out to Nellis via Keflavik, Goose Bay, Little Rock and Austin on the way out and Dallas, Trenton, Goose Bay and Keflavik on the way back. The only major event in the trail out and back was getting snowed in at Goose Bay on the way back. Each day involved getting up early and preparing the aircraft for the flight to Keflavik.

A weather window was needed to get into and out of Keflavik but it took five days before we were able to get out. The boredom quickly set in and as a form of entertainment we took to leaping out of second storey windows into the snow drifts but this quickly came to a halt when one of the locals pointed out that previous attempts at this had resulted in somebody finding a fire hydrant and ending up in hospital. As a more organised and safer way of amusing ourselves we arranged to go curling one afternoon but when we arrived at the ice rink the ice had melted (it was -32 degrees outside!) and we had to cancel the event.

Shortly after we returned from Vegas it was time for the postings to be announced as we were all moving back to the UK in a relatively short space of time. I got called into the WO's office and he welcomed me in and asked me where I wanted to go. I said north-east England would be my ideal choice but anywhere in central or eastern England would do (bearing in mind that probably covered about 75 per cent of the RAF in those days). He spluttered and grunted and opened his drawer just to check on the paperwork that what he was telling me was right. 'Oh well,' he said, 'you are going to 208 Squadron Buccaneers at RAF Lossiemouth in Northern Scotland.' It was disappointing but not a massive shock as all the Buccaneers were going there and it was obvious that a lot of us would be going as well.

I went home and told Dawn, who was also disappointed but not surprised. We started packing and prepared for our new life in the wild and woolly back of beyond.

Chapter 4

Lossiemouth

After driving for many hours and talking myself out of a speeding fine in Edinburgh, I arrived at the camp gates of RAF Lossiemouth. The local area didn't look too bad but the long drive through the mountains had made me wonder what it would be like when the weather was bad; I would find out on many occasions over the following years.

I arrived on 208 Squadron and met many familiar faces from Laarbruch and lots of new ones, too. It was easy to settle into the new surroundings and particularly the new job as I was already very experienced on the Buccaneer aircraft.

I marched into my married quarter, which was a maisonette in Lossiemouth village. Ideal location as I could walk or cycle to work in a few minutes. The house itself though left a lot to be desired. It was very run down and had pinkish carpets and green walls, and I was not sure how Dawn would take to it. As usual she took everything in her stride and soon set about trying to improve what we had. Having now been married for a few years and having had a good party tour of Germany, coupled with how difficult it was for English people to get a job in the local community, we decided that the time was right to start a family. Richard was born the following year in Mary Hill Hospital in Elgin.

The squadron originally operated from one of the hangars at Lossiemouth and the aircraft were towed out onto the line every day for flying to commence and were then towed back in each evening. This was a significant amount of work at the start and end of every day and so much different to operating out of hardened aircraft shelters (HAS) as we had done in Germany. I volunteered to do six months out of trade operating as a ramp tramp on the aircraft line, which was very enjoyable. I was responsible for making sure that all of the aircraft and see-off teams were ready for when the pilots walked for their aircraft and for making sure that everything went smoothly and any faults or problems were investigated and resolved with minimum disruption to the flying programme. It was a high-pressure job with lots of responsibility but one that I will always look back on as being one of the best I have had.

The nuclear weapon loading that we did so much of in Germany was also carried out at Lossiemouth but without using live weapons. The procedures were all the same regardless of whether we were using live or training weapons to ensure that standards were always extremely high. We were also still subjected to external checks to make sure our standards were high and did not deteriorate.

On one occasion we were halfway through a practice load when we noticed one of the external evaluators trying to sneak across the aircraft dispersal to where we were carrying out the weapon load. We knew that he would be coming to call a practice fire or practice emergency to test our speed and safety and as he continued to walk towards us we started to unplug and loosen the bomb rather than continue to load it. The evaluator got close and screamed at the top of his voice that there was a practice fire. We immediately lowered the bomb on its trolley and pulled it away from the aircraft in less than thirty seconds.

The evaluator was lost for words at the speed of our response and, although he congratulated us on our achievement, he implied that we had in some way cheated! As if!

HAS were being built at Lossiemouth but there was no estimate of when they would be completed or when each of the squadrons would be moving in. Once they were finished it was decided that we would go on a planned detachment to Gibraltar from the hangar and return to the HAS site. It worked very well and with so many ex Germany people on the squadron the transition from line operations to HAS operations was relatively painless.

During my two years on 208 Squadron we had several excellent detachments that took us all over the UK and Europe. There were regular trips to RAF St Mawgan in Cornwall to practise our deployability and maritime strike capability, plus trips to Denmark, Germany, Norway and Gibraltar.

At St Mawgan we operated on the far side of the airfield away from the main operational areas of the unit. On these exercises we tended to use a lot of chaff during the flying sorties. Chaff is a mix of fibreglass and aluminium fibres in bundles that interferes with all electronic equipment when released into the atmosphere. More modern aircraft had purpose-built dispensers for chaff but the Buccaneer was not so fortunate and it was the armourers' job to load it. This meant securing the chaff bundles to a sheet of plastic with heavy-duty tape and then taping the sheet on to the aircraft's airbrakes at the rear. On very early cold mornings you would get halfway along the line of aircraft and hear the thud from behind you as the tape came unstuck and the package dropped to the floor. You just hoped it had stayed intact and not burst open. The only way to prevent this was to have another team follow you along the line of aircraft with a hydraulic rig to close the airbrakes. On many occasions the aircrew would not use the chaff on their mission and as they returned to the airfield and broke into the circuit they would open the airbrake and black out the airfield for a short while until the chaff dispersed.

It was on one of the Gibraltar visits that due to a shortage of on-base accommodation for the junior ranks it was decided that an old Navy accommodation block at the opposite end of the Rock from the RAF base would be utilised for all corporals and below. The officers and SNCOs were living on base. The old Navy block was in a very poor state of repair but it did have a large function room in the cellar that could be utilised as a squadron bar. The officers and SNCOs purchased cans of beer for us from their messes at duty free rates to hold as stock and we sold it at no profit to those who wanted to use the bar. The senior corporals (of which I was one) were given the responsibility of policing the bar and ensuring that nobody drank in excess and that behaviour was good. However, we weren't always in the bar as we had to work and on some evenings we went into town so there was always the potential for misbehaviour.

One evening a few of us returned from town and on the way from the bus to the accommodation we heard screams and shouting, and it was obvious that something was going awry. As we entered the building we looked up three flights of stairs, where the screaming was coming from, and one of the Senior Aircraftsmen (SAC) had a beer barrel chained to his ankle and the barrel was just about to be hurled down the stairs by a group of airmen. We managed to stop them, re-briefed everybody on rules on behaviour and everything was calmed down with no harm coming to anybody.

A couple of nights later we were all sat around in the bar having a general chat when one of the mildest-mannered airmen you could ever wish to meet suddenly leapt out of his chair and started battering one of the other airmen. Something had obviously upset him and he must have had a bit too much to drink but nobody could ever have predicted what had just happened. We pulled him back and calmed the situation down and hoped that the incident would not escalate or get reported to anybody. The following day at work the flight sergeant pulled me and one of the other corporals to one side and gave us the most almighty rollicking that we had ever had. We tried to explain that nobody could have anticipated the incident but he was having none of it and marked our card for the rest of the detachment. On a previous detachment, the same flight sergeant had told us that we were Englishmen on a Scottish Squadron in Scotland and had better watch our steps. Our cards were indeed well and truly marked.

At the end of one of the Norway detachments all the squadron ground crew were invited to a leaving party that was hosted by our Norwegian counterparts. After several hours of drinking we decided to introduce the Norwegians to a game of spoons.

A brief outline of the rules of the game are as follows: Two players on opposing sides take it in turns to strike their opponent on the head with a spoon that is held in their mouth. The challenging or home team will have someone to supervise who, unbeknown to the challenger, will use a spoon in their hand to strike the away team head, therefore giving the opportunity for greater force to be applied. On this occasion, our supervisor had found a large ladle and was using it to strike the head of the Norwegian player. Usually, as you would expect, the team doing the hand striking will always win, but not on this occasion. The Norwegian player was so drunk he had no feeling and despite being struck on the head with a ladle he still managed to apply sufficient force with his mouth-held spoon to win the game. This was the first and only time I have seen the challenged player win a game of spoons.

Back at Lossiemouth another memorable moment came when one day when the squadron WO asked to see one of the armament corporals,

Corporal X, in his office. The corporal went in and was told he had been promoted and as expected he was over the moon and spent the rest of the day on the phone informing his friends and family. The following day the WO pointed to the corporal and said to his SNCO how pleased he was that Corporal X had been promoted. The SNCO looked at the Sqn WO and said, 'Sir, that is not Corporal X, that is Corporal Y.' The WO thought he was joking but once he realised that he was not they had to re-interview Corporal X to tell him of the mistake and then give the good news to Corporal Y.

A few weeks later I was called into the Squadron WO's office and he informed me that I also had been promoted. I was obviously over the moon (and hoped he had the right man this time) and was even further elated when he told me that with my promotion came a posting south. Where could it be? RAF Leeming? RAF Waddington? The options were vast. 'You are going to the Explosive Storage Area (ESA),' he said, which in fairness was about 200 yards south of the 208 Squadron HAS site. As my parting gift from 208 Squadron they gave me a passenger trip in a Hunter T7, which was as exhilarating as it gets as we thrashed around the low-flying areas of northern Scotland, did a few rollers (landing and taking off) at RAF Stornoway and made a simulated engine failure approach and landing back at Lossiemouth. A fantastic experience and another opportunity to use the in-flight sick bag.

I went away on my promotion courses (GST2 and TMT2) and arrived in the ESA as a just-turned 26-year-old sergeant. Realising that the only way to escape from Scotland was to apply to go to Germany again, my first job was to fill in the required forms and wait and hope for a posting to materialise. I was introduced to my work colleagues and taken around the site to see my new job. I was to take charge of the missile section of the ESA, which meant looking after Sidewinder, Martel TV and Martel AR missiles and the soon-to-be-introduced Sea Eagle. A very interesting and busy job in the early days but not enough to make me want to stay.

The majority of my spare time at Lossiemouth was taken up with golf in the summer months as a member of Moray Golf Club and skiing in the winter. Throughout the winter months a group of us would go skiing most weekends in the Cairngorms at either Aviemore or the Lecht. Often when we were on night shift we would go to the Lecht at 8 in the morning get a half-day skiing ticket, ski till 1 in the afternoon, drive home, get changed and go to work at 4.30 hoping and praying that it would not be a long night.

After about nine months I was told that I was to attend a Phantom aircraft weapons course at RAF Coningsby and would be posted to RAF Wildenrath in Germany at the end of the year. As my posting drew close I was given the obligatory send off from the ESA as they stripped me to my underpants, chained me to a bomb trolley, covered me in hand-cleansing gel and then hosed me clean with a fire hose. Not pleasant but not harmful. Time to pack up the house again with Dawn and Richard moving in with her parents while we waited for a married quarter.

Chapter 5

Wildenrath

I arrived at RAF Wildenrath to be informed that I would be working in Missile Servicing Flight (MSF) and would be in charge of a team of about ten working in the Movers Section. We lived and worked in a hardened building in the furthest corner of the missile site and we spent our time moving Sparrow, Skyflash and Sidewinder missiles around the unit, taking them to pieces for servicing and then rebuilding them. Again, not the most taxing of jobs but we had a great team and had some good fun. Highlight of the working day was playing bally, which was taking turns bouncing a large powerball off the building wall (outside) and if you failed to hit the wall on three occasions you were out of the game and had to buy a round of teas at the next tea break. If you had a bad week it could turn out quite expensive. On really quiet days when we had no missiles in the building we sometimes played five-a-side football in the building. That was until we got caught by the WO one day, who managed to glide all the way from his office to our building without being spotted, and more disturbingly without anybody warning us he was on his way. The door opened, he glided in and with a look of disdain on his face asked me to meet him in his office after tea break for a chat. The chat didn't go well and my card was marked.

After a couple of months, a married quarter (MQ) came available thirty minutes away in Teveren. I decided to take it and made arrangements for Dawn and Richard to fly out in time for Christmas. In the meantime, Dawn had found out she was pregnant again and this time with twins! In the following April, Dawn had an early morning rush to RAF Hospital Wegberg and Natalie and Sarah arrived before I could even get there, having dropped Richard off at playgroup. Life with the twins was hard and not made any easier living at Teveren, so I applied for an MQ on base at Wildenrath and got one fairly quickly.

This period of time was also seeing a resurgence of the IRA and in particular numerous terrorist attacks on mainland Europe against British Forces personnel. Everybody was in the habit of checking cars for bombs and booby traps if you left them anywhere off base. A car park full of cars with people an all fours checking the underside of their cars was as comical as it was terrifying. Two particular incidents spring to mind in these troubling times. On one occasion a corporal and his baby daughter were shot as they left the petrol station in Wildenrath village and both died at the scene. On another occasion three RAF Regiment gunners were shot in their car just across the border in Roermond in Holland. One of the Gunners died and the others were taken to RAF Hospital Wegberg at the same time as Dawn was preparing to be discharged after having the twins.

Another opportunity to go on Exercise Red Flag to Nellis came up with me and one of the JTs providing support to the deploying Phantom squadrons. Our main task was the preparation and supply of chaff and flares for the aircraft flying programme. One morning the JT was late out of bed and we made a mad dash to Nellis to get the chaff and flare magazines dispersed to each of the aircraft.

We took a short cut across the red line that bordered the aircraft parking dispersal and started to drop of the chaff and flare magazines at each of the aircraft. After about three aircraft loads we heard a rifle cock and somebody say, 'Sir, I need you to kneel down and put your hands on your head.' We obeyed the order and once they had confirmed that we were UK military, we were briefed on our misdemeanour of breaking the red line. The Squadron Engineering Officer had to sign a prisoner release chit to get us back off the US Air Force Police and we carried on with our duties. My brother was also on Exercise Red Flag at the time with XV Squadron Tornados from RAF Laarbruch and a colleague of his witnessed the whole event from the top of one of the aircraft that he was working on at the time. He had his camera with him (probably should have been arrested instead of me!) and took a photograph of me and the JT kneeling down with our hands on our head as we were under arrest.

As the two Phantom squadrons changed over halfway through the detachment, the VC10 aircraft that was swapping the personnel around announced that it was doing a weekend 'training' trip to Hickam Air

Force Base in Hawaii and that anybody who had some free time could go if they wanted to. The incoming ground crew were not allowed to go as they had to get ready for the next week's flying programme, and the outgoing ground crew were not allowed to go as they had to prepare to go home, so that only left the support staff. We had a great weekend in Hawaii, toured the island, stayed close to Waikiki Beach and visited Pearl Harbor. An excellent couple of days break and another opportunity to visit a prime location.

After a few weeks back at work I was told that my post was annotated as one that needed an Explosive Ordnance Disposal Course (EOD or Bomb Disposal) and that I had been nominated for a course at the end of the year. To be precise, it was the five weeks running up to Christmas and once again this didn't go down too well at home but duty called.

For the previous few months in MSF the Station EOD personnel had always either intrigued me or downright got on my nerves, driving around in tanks and pretending to be some sort of demigods and superior beings. Because of these feelings I left for my course with a great deal of trepidation. Did I want to be one of those knobs? Was I good enough? Could I pass the course that at the time, and still to this day, is one of the hardest in the military? I arrived at the Defence EOD School, in Chatham, Kent, met some old faces and knuckled down to the task in hand. I travelled back to Germany for a couple of the weekends that I was away sharing cars with a guy from RAF Bruggen. That meant a late Friday dash to the ferry and a late ferry back on the Sunday night ready to start first thing Monday morning. The course sailed by and we came to final test week, which thankfully I passed with flying colours but 50 per cent of the students failed: a figure that was the average then and isn't much better now. Back to Wildenrath in time for Christmas and a well-earned two-week break.

The EOD skills and way of life seemed to suit me both during routine training and on station exercises, and I was developing into a very competent EOD operator and team leader. So much so that when the EOD Continuation Training job came available in the station armoury I applied for it and got it. There was only me and an SAC in the EOD Training Cell and we were responsible for all the equipment, vehicles and continuation training for the unit's twelve EOD teams. To put this number in context, the twelve EOD teams that RAF Wildenrath had then is the same number as the entire RAF has today! The job was especially busy as it drew close to the annual sequence of exercises leading up to the Tactical Evaluation (TACEVAL) carried out by NATO.

We developed some excellent training scenarios and pushed the teams really hard but it always paid off with excellent grades being achieved from the TACEVAL team.

On one TACEVAL the Armoury WO was operating as a team leader in a Scimitar armoured vehicle. A couple of Belgian evaluators put out a large bomb with two fuzes in it and when the WO carried out his recce he identified both fuzes very quickly and went back to his vehicle to get his team to prepare the tools he needed. On approaching the bomb with his tools he noticed that the fuzes had changed and went back to his vehicle to prepare a new set of tools. On approaching the bomb for the second time the fuzes had changed again. By this time he was getting angry and instructed his driver to drive over the bomb and flatten it. His driver did so without question and as he reversed over it for the second time the Belgian evaluators came running over shouting and gesticulating as the expensive training bomb was now completely destroyed. The WO explained that it was not in TACEVAL rules to change fuzes mid-scenario and if they ever messed with him or any of his teams again he would run them over.

I was so taken with the whole EOD thing that I applied to be part of the NATO TACEVAL team and after carrying out a couple of exercises under supervision I qualified as an evaluator and that was something I carried on doing for the next twenty years or so.

The exercise season was in full swing and I had no time to travel back to the UK to do my Airfield EOD specialisation course as the station exercises were coming thick and fast. By the time I did get around to attending that course it was pretty much a walk in the park as I had been carrying out the specialisation on exercises for many months. At the time of attending the course it never even crossed my mind that later in life I would not only become an instructor on that course but also be the boss of the flight of personnel that delivered the training.

One of the most memorable TACEVALS that I took part in was at a Belgian Air Force base. The EOD evaluators for this event were mainly Germany-based UK personnel and when we turned up at the accommodation that had been pre-booked by the TACEVAL administration team there was an immediate problem with the number of rooms that had been booked. As it was late in the day there was nothing much that could be done so we ended up sharing hotel rooms with three to a room and two of us top and tailing in a double bed.

The evaluation itself went reasonably well except for on the first day, after the first air raid, one of the Belgian EOD teams turned up and due to a wrongly identified fuze they carried out an incorrect procedure that would have resulted in the loss of the team leader. We informed him of his demise and sent him home for forty-eight hours as a way of seeing if the unit could cope with the loss of one of its EOD teams. That night we came back for the next air raid and when the EOD team turned up it was the same team leader who had died earlier that day and should have been at home. They obviously thought that we would be working shifts and that we would not notice that they had put the same team out. We sent him home again and instructed the command team to carry on as normal but without that particular team. It materialised that they had very few teams in the Belgian Air Force and what they had basically moved around between units to take part in evaluations.

Every three months each of the RAF Germany units would send all of their unserviceable and life-expired explosives to a bombing range in Northern Germany where they were unpackaged and destroyed over the space of five days. All the units sent EOD personnel to carry out the demolition task and it always proved to be a fantastic experience on both a social and professional level. We used the opportunity to give newly qualified EOD personnel some valuable experience using different demolition techniques on a variety of ammunition types and also used the event to design, develop and trial demolition techniques on new weapons, ammunition and explosives. After a hard day's work on the range the team would always go out into the local town for some much-earned refreshment.

Whilst at Wildenrath it was rumoured that we would be taking part in a much-talked about, but seldom practised, Exercise Gillyflower. The station would be closed to flying for a few days and would be subjected to a full-blown simulated Cold War bombing raid practice scenario with all of the unit's EOD teams taking part. We would also be getting teams in from the EOD Unit at Wittering (what was to become 5131 (BD) Sqn) to assist with the exercise and demonstrate their deep-buried bomb capability.

With twelve EOD teams taking part from the unit we were supposed to be able to clear the unit's aircraft operating surfaces in four hours in order to allow flying operations to recommence. We achieved the aim with five minutes to spare and received many plaudits for our hard work and professionalism. However, the most memorable moment was watching the RAF Wittering team demonstrate their deep-buried bomb, locating and excavating capability. Prior to the exercise we had buried a 1,000lb practice bomb in the training area and all the EOD personnel gathered around to witness the capability being displayed. They could not locate the bomb so the Armoury WO mimicked water divining with a piece of twig and indicated where the bomb should be. They took the hint and started using their location equipment in that area and got a reading on the equipment that indicated where the bomb was. They started to dig using heavy excavating equipment, which was supposed to get them close to the bomb, before using manual equipment to carry out the uncovering of the bomb. After an hour or so the digger struck the bomb and then pulled it out in a bucket of soil.

The watching teams from Wildenrath could do nothing but laugh at such an amateurish performance from the 'professionals'.

Another part of my job in the training cell was to deliver EOD briefs to all new arrivals on the station. This brief explained to them primarily what EOD teams did on the station, what we did on exercises and what we expected station personnel to do to assist us. To improve this experience, we got authority to develop a power of explosives demonstration to show all new arrivals in conjunction with the classroom brief. We did several trials to ensure that everything would work as designed and that safety distances were sufficient for the spectators. Whilst carrying out one of these trials we were simulating an anti-personnel cluster munition going of under someone's foot as if they had stood on it. We used an old boot filled with sand and a small amount of plastic explosive. We did not take into consideration which way the boot was facing and it flew towards us at great speed, landing just a few feet short. After the nervous laughter had settled down we recalculated the distances and direction and logged them into our memory bank so as not to make such a mistake again. The demonstrations were carried out on a weekly basis for the next few years and all went off without incident.

On another occasion we were delivering briefs to station personnel about the importance of checking vehicles prior to driving them as the IRA were extremely active at the time. As part of the brief we showed people a simulation of an under-car booby trap bomb that could operate as either a timed device or as a motion-sensitive device. As we introduced this bomb to the audience we set it in timing mode with a sound unit fitted (a simulated detonator that made a large bang) placed it to one side and carried on with the brief. After a couple of minutes, the timer counted down, the electrical circuit was made and sound unit went off, scaring the majority of the audience. Point made with great effect and everybody saw the funny side of the incident, and more importantly the very real simplicity with which these devices could be made and placed on to vehicles. Everybody that is except for one Chief Tech, who proceeded to bollock me for not warning people that there was going to be a large bang and pointing out that some people could have hearing problems and would be affected by the noise. I pointed out that warning people would lessen the impact of the brief and that as we were all operating on a Cold War footing in Germany, as well as having active IRA terror cells in the region, if anybody was that sensitive to noise they probably shouldn't be in the military. Needless to say, he didn't share my point of view and carried on bollocking me.

It was also our job to assist with building and igniting the station bonfire on 5 November and one year was particularly unforgettable. It was raining and miserable as we assisted the station working party to build the bonfire, making sure it was in the right place and properly constructed to allow us access for the ignition charges. We intended to place three, 5-litre plastic containers filled with fuel around the bonfire and ignite them using detonating cord. Because of the inclement weather we decided to put a bit of fuel onto the fire as well so that it would soak into the damp wood and make ignition easier. The fuel tanker driver was squirting the fuel on and after couple of minutes he asked if that was enough as he had used 500 litres!

We looked at each other as that was probably a bit much but there was nothing we could do about it now and it was still a good few hours until the bonfire lighting so it would hopefully evaporate. It came to ignition time and a station dignitary was invited to press the button to ignite the fire. We've all been to bonfires where they are ignited with a pop and a small flame appears in the middle and after a few minutes you have a raging bonfire that burns for hours after the fireworks have finished. This was different: loud bang, instant raging inferno and the fire was smouldering embers within thirty minutes. Spectacular, loved by all who attended and immense relief for me and the team.

One day we were sat in the training cell building that was just over the road from the station armoury and the station fire alarm sounded and over the loudspeaker system it said there was a fire in the armoury. We looked at one another assuming it was a practice but as we looked across the road smoke was coming from the roof of the main armoury building. There had been some contractors working in the loft space earlier and they had been welding a leaking water pipe but they had now left.

The smoke got thicker and a lot of fire engines turned up from both the station and the local community. After some discussion they decided to chop into the roof to gain access to the fire. As they did so the air rushed in and the fire went from a small and localised fire to a raging inferno that filled the entire roof cavity.

The Station Regiment Officer arrived with his incident commander's hat and jacket on, assessed the situation and began to take control. As you would expect, there was a lot of valuable aircraft equipment in the armoury but he decided that the guns were the most important (well he was a Regiment Officer) and sent several of us into the gun store to pull out what we could. The smoke was thick and black and we got a couple of the mobile trollies out before he told us to withdraw. Then he changed his mind and he told us to go back in but by then it was too dangerous and everything else perished in the fire. The armoury was completely destroyed and had to relocate into another vacant building on the unit over the coming weeks. Every SNCO who had an equipment inventory quickly listed all the things that had been missing and declared that they had been lost in the fire. There was nearly as much stuff lost in the fire as there was when the *Atlantic Conveyor* sank during the Falklands conflict.

After the fire a few of us were referred to the medical centre for a check-up because of smoke inhalation and as none of us had any lasting damage we decided to go to the bowling alley for a drink to sooth our throats. That night was registration night for the new intersection bowling league. We entered a team and won the league that year.

An opportunity arose to travel to RAF Gatow in Berlin on one of the station's Andover aircraft to deliver some training on the aircraft emergency signal pistol. Nobody from the small arms section wanted to go (it was their job) as they didn't see the point of going to Berlin for one night. This was a historic time as the Berlin Wall had just come down so I volunteered for the trip. I had a quick refresher on how to use the signal pistol, went home to pack my overnight bag and went to get on to the flight.

After the short flight to Gatow I delivered the training to half a dozen personnel and was shown to my accommodation. I got changed, threw my bag on the bed and went into Berlin by taxi. We walked the streets visited some bars and walked sections of the wall that had by now been destroyed. We returned to Gatow the following morning, got changed and went to board our return flight to Wildenrath. A good night out in Berlin was had at a momentous time in history.

The intersection football league in RAF Germany was of a very high standard and became a way of life for most of the people who played in it. The armourers' team was a combined one from both MSF and the station armoury and was reasonably good. We were able to hold our own against most teams and even managed to pull off some surprise results from time to time. The highlight of my few years there playing football was reaching the cup final but sadly we lost to the Aircraft Servicing Flight.

Some months earlier it had been announced that RAF Wildenrath would be closing as part of Options for Change. The manning team from the UK had travelled out to Wildenrath to brief everybody on options for posting, noted everybody's preferences and took them back to the UK to formulate a plan. With the kids still being young we decided it would be nice if we could get to RAF Leeming, close to both sets of grandparents and the ideal location and time to have our family around us. After a few weeks the manning people called and offered me postings to either Manston or St Mawgan; the two opposite corners of England to where we wanted to be. However, they pointed out, there was a vacancy for an EOD qualified Sergeant at RAF Gutersloh (Germany) if I was interested.

We had recently carried out a TACEVAL on RAF Gutersloh and had given them a marginal rating for their EOD teams' performance so I saw this as some form of karma. I accepted the Gutersloh posting with a promise that I would be there for three years and was told to attend a Harrier weapons course back in the UK prior to arriving. That done I returned to Wildenrath to pack up the house for another move. I phoned the flight sergeant at Gutersloh to get some details and he told me that as soon as I arrived I would be going on a two-week field deployment with the Harrier Force as an EOD team leader. I questioned this course of action as I had no understanding of Harrier operations or field deployments but he told me that I had given them sub-standard marks on their exercise and therefore they were deploying more teams and I would be on one of those teams. House packed, it was off to Gutersloh.

Chapter 6

Gutersloh

I arrived at Gutersloh and picked up a speeding fine on day one as I drove up to the camp gate. I arrived at the station armoury and was shown to my new workplace, which was affectionately known as the 'No Gun, No Pod Bay'. When the Harrier GR.3 was in service the gun and pod bay was a bustling busy workplace servicing all the 30mm Aden guns and gun pods that the aircraft carried. However, the GR.5 did not yet have a gun that worked and therefore the gun pods were just items of the airframe that helped the aircraft hover. There were very few, if any, spares, therefore there was nothing to service.

As my first experience with Harrier aircraft progressed it soon became clear to me that the 'Harrier Force', as it liked to be known, was not as joined up, punchy or operational as it liked to think it was. I began to refer to it as the 'Harrier Farce' and the name stuck so much that it was even engraved on my leaving gift at the end of my tour.

This could have resulted in a very boring working environment, however the saving grace was that my bay also covered the Harrier Servicing Flight (HSF) and every new GR.5 aircraft that was received from the manufacturer had an in-depth service prior to being released on to the flying squadrons. It was during one of these servicings that we experienced a great deal of difficulty in removing the ejection seat main gun from the aircraft cockpit. The bolts were extremely difficult to get out and needed some gentle persuasion with a hammer whilst wobbling the gun backwards and forwards to try and free it (this was standard practice with all gun removals). Eventually the bolt came out and we removed the gun and took it with all of the seat equipment to the seat bay for servicing.

A few hours later we received a call saying that the airframes tradesmen had discovered damage on the bottom seat gun bracket in the cockpit. They had consulted the Engineering Officer and the British Aerospace representative in HSF, who declared that the bracket was beyond repair and would have to be replaced. These brackets were extremely rare and therefore it was likely that the aircraft would be out of service for several months. This news didn't go down well with the senior management on the unit and they instigated a unit inquiry to identify the cause and apportion blame. The following day the British Aerospace representative found a bracket in his drawer and the aircraft was repaired, the servicing was completed and the aircraft was back with the squadron before the unit inquiry had even started. My own investigation into the aircraft tolerance limits highlighted that the tolerances for the bracket and the bolt were such that they could both be the same size, and instead of using grease they used some sort of sticky compound that seemed to seal the bolts in place. All of this pointed to problems in the manufacturing and assembly process but it was decided that me and my team were negligent and we were given a reprimand.

The other diversion and part of routine life at Gutersloh, of course, were the Harrier field deployments, for which I was pre-warned. The first one occurred not long after I arrived and I met with my EOD team to carry out some training and prepare our vehicle and equipment for the deployment. Our deployment vehicle was a canvas topped 4-ton truck that was kitted out to a high spec with bunk beds, a fridge (for x-ray machine film – and beer) and sufficient electrical infrastructure to run a TV as well. A large workbench doubled as the bed for the third member of the team by throwing a rather grotty looking mattress on top of it at bed time.

We found out that we were deploying to RAF Wildenrath but would be living in the woods and not allowed to use any of the station infrastructure. We drove to Wildenrath and set up our hide in the woods along with all of the aircraft and support personnel for Flying Site 1. In hindsight, it was a great experience and my team was excellent. The weather was atrocious with rain and high winds for much of the two weeks that we were away. A bus was laid on in the middle weekend to take people back to Gutersloh but as a team we decided not to bother as we were in the zone and filthy so did not fancy getting clean and comfortable to come back to the developing swamp a couple of days later. The winds and rain over the weekend tore down shelters and sent the portable toilets cartwheeling across the site, all very unpleasant, especially the tidy up process. My second deployment was to Sennelager for the TACEVAL where the weather was better and the teams were all on top of their game and we passed with a good grading.

Following on from my footballing success at Wildenrath, the Gutersloh Armoury football team was also of a good standard that managed its fair share of wins. During one of the games I badly hurt my leg and that injury still plagues me to this day. We also got a reputation for having the fattest midfield in RAF Germany with me and my fellow midfielders relying more on skill than speed. I played in several positions over the two seasons I was there with my most memorable match being one in which I played centre forward. I scored three goals, split my mouth open in a collision with the goalkeeper and was substituted, all in the first sixty minutes.

The armoury sent a small team to Deci to support a Harrier detachment and they needed a sergeant to oversee the team. None of the bay sergeants were available so I volunteered. It was a fairly uneventful detachment, the highlight of which was the opportunity to go to a football match between Cagliari and AC Milan. A few of us decided it was too good an opportunity to miss and got the MT bus to drop us off close to the stadium in Cagliari. We managed to buy some tickets off a bloke in a bar and walked to the stadium in good time to have a drink and soak up the atmosphere. We were in the home fans' end, which made the atmosphere even more intense, especially when Cagliari scored after only ten minutes. It was still 1-0 at half time but not long after the second half started AC Milan equalised and then scored three more goals in quick succession. Nobody should have been surprised as this was the AC Milan team with Ruud Gullit, Frank Rijkaard and Marco van Basten playing for them and van Basten scored three times.

The atmosphere changed very quickly and the home fans started to riot, while the away fans started ripping up the plastic seats and launching them into the home fans on the tier below. The final whistle sounded and the violence spilled on to the streets outside the stadium with cars being overturned and running battles in the streets. Of course, as the media would have us believe, football violence is a very British thing and here were five Brits in the middle of a war zone wondering how the white

RAF MT bus would be able to get in, pick us up, and get out again? Miraculously it did and we all returned safely to RAF Decimomannu.

Not long after returning from Deci the next stage of the RAF Germany draw down was announced and this included the closure of RAF Gutersloh, with all personnel and aircraft being transferred to RAF Laarbruch. I was told it was likely that my three-year posting would be cut to two. Once the draw down dates started to be finalised the manning people from the UK came out to brief and interview everybody (similar to what they did at Wildenrath). I was told that my posting could be cut even more, which was a bit disappointing as I had moved from Wildenrath with my family hoping for a bit of stability. It was not to be and my tour was cut to eighteen months but I did manage to secure a posting to RAF Leeming as previously hoped for; it was just eighteen months later than I'd originally wanted and via a tour at Gutersloh.

The house and car, wife and kids were packed up again and we were off to RAF Leeming.

Chapter 7

Leeming

I arrived at RAF Leeming station armoury full of the joys of spring. We had at last got a posting close to our parents so babysitting would no longer be an issue and it was also nice for the grandparents to be able to see their grandchildren a bit more often. I was also taking up an EOD training role again, although this time shared with another sergeant and an SAC. There was a lot of EOD training to be done as the exercise programme was still in full flow and in addition to this training and exercise burden, RAF Leeming was also doing weekly clearance at Cowden bombing range, which was on the east coast just north of Hull. There was also a rumour that we would be taking over the monthly clearance task of the Wiley Sike bombing range at RAF Spadeadam from 5131 (BD) Sqn. A busy time ahead.

I had been a sergeant for coming up to eight years by this time and promotion had slowed down dramatically right across the RAF due mainly to the reduction in overall manpower. I started to look at other options for enhancing my career options and make life a bit more challenging, and I decided that commissioning was the way ahead. I was only a few years away from my 35th birthday, the minimum age for taking a commission through the branch officer route, and I already had the required qualifications so decided that this would be my new focus in life. I applied for a place on an RAF Leeming pre-commissioning course, which was a week-long preparation course to see if you had what it took to make that leap and at least give you a head start in the application process.

We did a couple of days of classroom work; some team-building exercises and practice interviews and then went for a day of fitness training/assessment. After a morning of navigation exercises and speed marching around Catterick ranges we headed off back to Leeming via Catterick Garrison, where we ran around the airfield, did the confidence (assault) course and then ran back around the airfield to the gymnasium.

Halfway back to the gym I got excruciating cramp in one of my legs and had to stop running. I was given a lift back to the gym in the back of a Land Rover, got showered and changed and then we returned to Leeming. The following day we returned to the education centre for a debrief and I was debriefed by a rather large female flight lieutenant who told me that although my academic abilities were good I was not fit enough for the commissioning process and should give up on my dream. I pointed out that if I had known we were going to do a physical hell day I would have trained for it. She remained unimpressed and said she doubted I would ever make it. Thanks for that! To be continued ...

Shortly after arrival at Leeming I was sent on an RAF instructors' course that lasted for two weeks and took place at RAF Newton. The course was very intensive and informative, and as it was carried out before the general roll out of PowerPoint all presentations were done on overhead projector slides and using cut out cardboard models for demonstrations. It was this painstaking and labour-intensive preparation that necessitated the two-week course.

The course changed titles regularly during the early years; from Basic Instruction Techniques (BIT) to Defence Instruction Techniques (DIT) but it was the Trade Instruction Techniques title that lasted for the shortest amount of time!

Following on from the instructors' course several of us were sent to RAF Halton to attend a first aid instructors' course. This was becoming a vital role as all EOD teams had been told that they must have extra first aid training and specifically trauma training for when they were working on remote ranges and clearance sites.

The time came for us to take over the Wiley Sike clearance task from 5131 (BD) Sqn and a couple of us travelled to Spadeadam to get the handover brief. We were taken out onto the bombing target and the 5131 (BD) Sqn SNCO explained that all attacking aircraft came onto the range from the west and that it was this direction of travel that we should base our clearance task on. At this point we looked at each other and wondered what sort of handover brief we were getting. All of the holes in the target indicated that attacks were coming from the south.

We then went to see the explosive storage facility, which he told us was in the guardroom. That seemed odd, but we went to look anyway.

The explosive licence in the guardroom stated that it was for small arms ammunition only and, additionally, we knew from experience that you needed to have separate storage facilities for plastic explosive and detonators. He said that it was OK to use it as we were only there once a month. We knew this to be untrue, took over the site and then sorted everything out properly.

For carrying out the range clearance task we had two options open to us: one was to do the trip in a day taking the explosives with us, and the other was for us to stay the night close to the range and park the van with explosives in a local police station or military storage facility in Carlisle. It was decided that the second option was the preferred one and that is what we did every month from then on.

On one of the clearance days we were told that flying had finished for the day and therefore we drove out to the target to carry out the clearance. We found a couple of unexploded practice bombs and checked with range control to confirm that flying was complete before we set our explosive charges. They confirmed that it was so we set our charges and lit the time fuse with a ten-minute delay to allow us to get clear of the range. At the seven-minute point a Harrier aircraft came flying over the range very low and heading for the target area. Our hearts were in our mouths and we quickly tried to make radio contact with range control but there was no answer. The aircraft could be seen circling the range and coming around for another attack, but we had no way of alerting the pilot and communications with the range control were not working. The Harrier overflew the target again and thirty seconds later the charges went off, kicking debris high into the air, well above the height the aircraft had been at. On returning to range control we reported the incident to try and ascertain why the aircraft had ignored the no-fly zone and why the range controllers had not warned the aircraft but nothing ever came of it.

The weekly Cowden clearance task was becoming quite a burden on the unit and had come about primarily because the sergeant at RAF Staxton Wold had medical issues that prevented him from carrying out the task and therefore RAF Leeming was tasked to do it for a few months. The sergeant EOD post at Staxton Wold was eventually disestablished once it was confirmed that we could take the task on permanently.

The job involved an early start for a three-man team picking up the explosives and then driving the two hours to RAF Cowden in our V8 Ford Transit van. Once at Cowden we would wait for the flying programme to cease, as the range was still operational at that time, and then made our way onto the beach. Like a lot of the East Yorkshire coastline, the cliffs at RAF Cowden were eroding at quite a fast rate and access to the beach was via a different route each time. It was literally a case of finding a route to scramble down the cliff and then scramble back up when we had finished. The beach was often littered with practice bombs that were either being washed up from the sea or falling onto the beach as the cliff eroded. Many of the bombs would be expended and therefore pose no danger but due to the amount of time they had been in the water or soil it was impossible to tell. Therefore, the only way to make sure was to blow them apart with plastic explosive therefore rendering them safe. Due to the remoteness of our location we would use pyrotechnic time fuse to initiate the charges.

On one particular trip we set off as normal and arrived in good time, but the range was still open so we had some lunch and watched the aircraft bombing out at sea and strafing the land targets. The tide times were going to be quite tight if we didn't get on to the beach soon. Eventually the range closed and we made our way down the cliff carrying all of our equipment and explosives. One of the non-EOD qualified training cell personnel had come with us on this occasion as our safety man and as he made his way down the cliff he dropped the bag of explosives down a crevice in the cliff. After a great deal of laughing about how this could happen we set about trying to recover them and after about fifteen minutes we succeeded and made our way down onto the beach, but it was obvious that the tide had turned and was on its way back in at a fair rate of knots. We decided to place charges on any suspect items as we made our way along the beach, light the time fuse and then check them all on the way back to save time.

As we got to the end of the range limits everything had so far detonated as planned and it would just be a case of checking the remnants on the way back once the final charge had gone off. Our faith was misplaced as the final charge did not go off. The standard procedure for such an event was to wait a set amount of time equivalent to three times the length if the time fuse plus another thirty minutes. On this occasion that amount of waiting time was not going to be possible due to the waves already lapping around our ankles, so we waited as long as we decided it was safe to do so and went back and placed another charge next to the one that had not gone off. We waited till the charge went off and then quickly checked what we could of the previous charges before making our way to the top of the cliff.

On arriving back at the air traffic control tower, we noticed that a Ford Sierra in the car park had a broken rear window and there was the tail of a 28lb practice bomb sitting on the parcel shelf. One of our explosions had sent the tail unit up and over the cliff and through the back window of the car. It was one of those situations that looked impossible but, as I would come to learn throughout my career, when you are having a bad day anything can happen. We reported the incident and set off back to RAF Leeming with some stories to tell for that day.

Operation Deny Flight was called in response to the horrors that were occurring in the Balkans and it soon became clear that RAF Leeming's Tornado F3 squadrons would be deploying to assist in policing the no-fly zone over the region. The first squadron deployed to Gioia del Colle in Italy and started flying operations within days. A full support team had also deployed at very short notice and within a few months it was time to rotate those personnel. I sort of volunteered to be the armament detachment leader for the next rotation and soon me and my team were off to Gioia.

The lads were all living in a run-down barrack block on base and I was put up in a hotel in a local town with the other detachment SNCOs. It soon became apparent that more personnel would be deploying as the Jaguar Force joined in with the operation and the base accommodation was no longer going to be suitable for the amount of people deploying. And so began a race to see who could get the best accommodation that would still allow daily travel to work.

Eventually all of the Tornado F3 detachment would be accommodated in a holiday villa complex on the coast at Monopoli. This accommodation was outstanding with swimming pool, tennis courts and sports pitches. However, the long drive to work coupled with twenty-four-hour cover being needed often meant that a two-shift system would become draining on personnel. We therefore adopted a three-shift system (using the same amount of manpower) that made work time a bit harder but with more down time it became more bearable.

It was one of those occasions that occur early in operations where all peacetime rules and regulations cannot be met so you just get by using your experience and trying to keep operating as safely as possible at all times. For our explosive storage and preparation area we had been given one hardened aircraft shelter (HAS) in a HAS site close to the end of the runway. In that HAS we stored all the air-to-air missiles and components, all aircraft ammunition, chaff, flare and all other ancillary explosive items as well as ground equipment, tools and paperwork. It was effectively a fully functioning missile servicing flight and ESA all in one building. A great detachment with an outstanding, hard-working team. After four months in Italy it was back to RAF Leeming and time for me to submit my commissioning paperwork. This went through fairly quickly and in the process I had interviews with my flight commander and the Station Commander and passed with flying colours. It was now a case of sitting and waiting for the next phase.

In parallel with submitting my paperwork I decided that I had better take some action to improve my fitness levels as I had struggled during the commissioning course week. I was still playing football, squash and golf but needed to improve my aerobic fitness and stamina and decided that running was going to be the only way to achieve this. I threw myself fully into a training regime regularly running 3 and 5-mile routes with the occasional 8-mile run thrown in.

In the meantime, I was nominated for a Tornado course at RAF Cottesmore in order to expand my reducing EOD role into weapon load training and second-line servicing in ASF. Whilst on the Tornado course I was informed that I had been nominated to attend the Officer and Aircrew Selection Centre (OASC) as the final phase of the commissioning selection process and that I had six weeks to prepare. As the only person living on base on my Tornado course (all the others were daily commuting from RAF Coningsby) it gave me the perfect opportunity to prepare myself fully. Every evening I went to the sergeants' mess ante-room and read every single newspaper from cover to cover, as well as many of the key periodicals, and by the end of the five-week course my general knowledge and current affairs knowledge were second to none. I returned to Leeming and the following week went to RAF Cranwell for the selection process. I was a bag of nerves throughout the two days but obviously performed well as a few weeks later I was notified that I had been successful and would be starting Initial Officer Training (IOT) in a month or so.

The whole flash to bang time was very quick for me, with OASC taking place in August and me starting IOT in October. Dawn and the kids were happy as they would be able to stay in our MQ at Leeming for the duration of IOT and I would be able to get home at weekends if the IOT training programme allowed.

Chapter 8

Cranwell

I arrived at RAF Cranwell on a Sunday afternoon and was checked in at the guardroom and directed to my accommodation block. We were living in one of the old blocks in two-man rooms with each individual flight being assigned to a leg of the building. Somebody with a sense of humour had decided it would be a good idea to pair me (ex-SNCO armourer) with an Oxford University graduate who had degrees in maths and physics and all of the social skills associated with being at university. Despite our vastly differing background and levels of intelligence, we got on very well once we had sorted out a few ground rules: number one being that you do not go to the bar until you have finished your personal admin and domestic chores. It took him a while to get the idea but we got there eventually.

On the first day of physical training we were all grouped together and sent off on a one-and-a-half-mile streaming run. The procedure was fairly simple in that the result of the run would determine which fitness training group you would be in for the duration of IOT. The first third would be in group A, the second third in group B and the final third in group C. I was advised before I went to Cranwell to try and get into group B, as group A were the gym monkeys who were super fit and super competitive; group C were the less fit and were often given a hard time by the PTIs to get them to a much-improved level, with group B being those of a reasonable level that only had to avoid being dropped into group C. I followed this advice and managed to get myself into the middle of the pack.

Our flight commander was an RAF Regiment Officer who had, in his previous life, been a grave digger. He was very strict and straight laced and did not suffer fools gladly, but he was also very fair. We were not allowed off camp for the first four weeks and then it came to the four-week block and kit inspection, the result of which would determine if we would be allowed out for the weekend (my first chance to go home). As our room got inspected the course adjutant called my name and my heart sank. I was summoned to my locker, where he was standing holding my West Ham United tie. He asked me if I thought it was becoming of being an officers' tie, he clearly did not, so I agreed with him and agreed to hide it out of the way. We passed the inspection and were allowed out on Saturday morning but had to be back on Sunday night, plenty of time to get to RAF Leeming and back. I later discovered that the adjutant was a Manchester United supporter and hated West Ham, hence his dislike for my tie.

Our flight was an eclectic mix of individuals who quickly came together as a team. As with all situations like this, everybody has their own view on what teamwork and co-operation meant and looked like. One person in particular was a chap from the Jamaican Defence Force (JDF) who had a very Jamaican view on life in that everything was laid back and no job or task should be hurried. That outlook, coupled with a view that communication was a one-way thing (you had to tell him but he didn't have to tell you), led to some very interesting situations.

On one occasion there was a lot of banging and clashing in the corridor outside our rooms in the early hours of the morning. Investigation highlighted that our JDF colleague was ironing his uniform. When asked what he thought he was up to ironing at three in the morning he pointed out that other people made noise when he liked to sleep in the early evening so he thought he was doing nothing wrong. We pointed out the error of his ways and in the end he conceded that he might have been wrong.

On another occasion we were sat in the classroom when the flight commander pointed out that one of the flight was wearing civilian black socks with patterns on them and as we all looked at one another and checked, it became apparent that the JDF chap was indeed wearing patterned socks. When asked why he stated that he had no clean plain black socks and thought the patterned ones would be OK for the day. The whole flight was punished with homework of writing an essay on the need for teamwork and the importance of checking one another for uniform conformity.

The essay just confirmed, for him, that it was everybody's fault but his that he was improperly dressed.

Spread across the whole course were quite a few ex-rankers from all walks of service life and the IOT flight commanders relied on these individuals to use their knowledge and experience to organise the flights and whip the others into shape. It was a system and ethos that seemed to work with a lot being achieved in a short space of time in the early days.

The officers' mess associated with our accommodation was closed for refurbishment so we had to be bussed to the OASC candidates' mess for every meal. This additional travel requirement added a large chunk of time to every meal and when you build in the self-generated additional five minutes before everything 'just in case' it led to some very long days.

A normal daily routine would be up at 0530, bus to breakfast 0615, bus back from breakfast 0715, finish jobs and tidy up before forming up outside the block to march across for lessons at 0800. Lunchtime routine was bus to lunch and bus back, therefore no spare time in the block to catch up on any admin, and dinner would be bus to the mess then bus back, getting back to the block at 1830ish and having to start on admin and block cleaning jobs. This went on for about ten weeks before our mess reopened, making life a bit easier. After sixteen weeks we did our final leadership camp at STANTA training area in Norfolk and those who passed moved across to College Hall Officers' Mess for the final eight weeks. This accommodation was single-man rooms with the mess being in the same building, and although still intensive it was far more enjoyable. The miracle was that in those first sixteen weeks my roommate and I had become good friends, with a good understanding of one another, and I had not killed him. He was without doubt one of the cleverest people I have ever met but he just lacked some common sense and an ability to prioritise what was really important.

It was during IOT that I got the opportunity for another air experience flight and this time in a Bulldog training aircraft. Many of the IOT students came from University Air Squadrons and had many hours flying Bulldog aircraft, therefore the flying opportunities were offered to those who had not previously flown in that type. Again, a great opportunity for me to experience something new and this time I managed to come back without having to use the little blue sick bag.

We were asked after week sixteen to put our posting choices in and all that I was really bothered about was getting an Officer Commanding Armament Engineering Flight (OC AEF) job and didn't really mind where it was. I was doing some preparation for a presentation and needed some information from my friends in the armoury at Leeming. I rang the armoury and got the information that I needed and the conversation turned to postings. They had heard that I was being posted to RAF Leuchars (the other half of the Tornado F3 Force) as OC AEF, which I was pleased about but would rather hear it through official channels as I had been around long enough to know that rumours weren't always right. A few weeks later the manning people (yes those again) came to let us know where we were going. I was told that it was against their better judgement to give me an armament post but they had been persuaded to do so and that they were posting me to RAF Leuchars. I explained that I thought the idea of having branch officers was for them to continue operating in their specialist area and that the posting suited me and the armament world. I was then told that after my two years at Leuchars I would be going to the Falkland Islands for six months, again I took this with a pinch of salt as manning were normally incapable of planning more than three months ahead and the chance of them getting a two-year plan off the ground was remote. Or so I thought!

It was then time for Exercise Peacekeeper, which was a field exercise held at RAF Barkston Heath. We all took turns in leading various elements of the base from the headquarters (HQ) to the guard force, domestic duties to roving armed patrols. It was well known that on the final night of the exercise there would be a huge ground attack with lots of blank ammunition being fired. As expected, the attack happened and the night sky was lit up with flashes and bangs. The young and enthusiastic cadets were firing like there was no tomorrow and were quickly running out of ammunition, so I gave them some of mine. The following day we returned to Cranwell and sat outside the armoury cleaning our weapons before handing them in. Each weapon was meticulously inspected by the armoury staff and on 95 per cent of the occasions given back to the individual for further cleaning. I handed mine in without any problem and later I was asked how I had cleaned my weapon so quickly to such a high standard. I explained that I had given most of my ammunition away to those who wanted it, therefore my weapon didn't get very dirty. I had also brought with me some new spare parts to replace the really dirty items on my rifle.

Those who had passed the exercise and therefore passed IOT were informed of their success and those that had not were re-coursed to try the phases again. Lots of drill practice and uniform preparation was now the order of the day in preparation for the graduation ceremony. On the day of the graduation parade the sun was shining and Dawn and my parents were in attendance as I marched up the steps of College Hall Officers' Mess (CHOM). Flying Officer Haygarth, soon to be OC Arm at RAF Leuchars. Another proud moment.

IOT was followed immediately by attending the five-week Engineering Common Management Module of EOT2, also at Cranwell, before returning to Leeming, packing up the house and family for the drive north and to move into our MQ at Leuchars.

Chapter 9

Leuchars

I arrived at RAF Leuchars for my first commissioned tour and it was to be a steep learning curve graduating from a bloke who used to work in the armoury to one who was now running the show (apart from the WO obviously). Having come from one Tornado F3 unit to another, the adjustment was fairly easy as I knew what each of the working bays did and therefore it was just a case of adapting to the different working practices. The people in the armoury were fantastic and did everything they could to make my life as easy as possible.

One of the big differences was the routine weekly meetings with the squadron commander and cascading that information to the flight. In a short space of time I was standing in for him at OC Engineering Wing meetings as part of my personal development. Again, this was an eye-opener for me getting to understand what all of the other flights and squadrons did in such detail. It was also a culture shock in that I now had to look at the bigger picture, be less of a shop steward and more of a politician.

The officers' mess at Leuchars was a thriving entity with the majority of members living either in the mess or in married quarters, and with regular functions and weekly happy hours it was a great place to be.

Being so close to St Andrews was also a massive bonus for the golfers and I saw this as my opportunity to take my 'once in a blue moon' golf-playing habits to another level. I joined the station golf society and just that tiny step came with great benefits. For £150 per year you got to play all the six courses at St Andrews (including the legendary Old Course) as often as you liked. As an officer, you also got honorary membership of the Royal & Ancient Golf Club (the R&A) and with it all of the benefits of the wonderful clubhouse overlooking the Old Course. Very soon I was playing for the Station Commander's golf team against the R&A itself. The Station Commander at Leuchars was also Air Officer Scotland

and Northern Ireland (AOSNI) and was therefore an Air Commodore. In the space of six months I had gone from being a sergeant at RAF Leeming to having post-golf match dinner either in the R&A or in the Air Commodore's house. My golf improved immensely during my time at Leuchars with evening games in the summer, weekend league games, golf society away days and the occasional social game with the guys from work. On many occasions the guys would book a tee time on the Old Course and after the game I would take them into the R&A for something to eat and drink. A fantastic opportunity for me to able to do this for the guys who were all mad keen golfers.

This sort of regular activity highlighted to the non-golfers in the armoury that there was a golfing clique forming and, even worse, the Boss was part of it. The golfers were having time off work to play golf and the non-golfers, particularly the hill walkers, were revolting.

I decided that it was time to put this imbalance right and told the non-golfers (who were mainly Munro bagging hill walkers) that they could also have time off work to go on properly organised walking events. For the uninitiated, Munro bagging is the act of climbing as many Munros as possible and ticking them off a list. A Munro is a hill/mountain over 3,000ft high.

They got together and started to organise regular walking trips in and around the local mountains and decided to ask me along to one of their jaunts. I decided that for the good of the team and for armoury cohesion I would go along. We spent the best part of three hours walking to the top of a mountain and as we reached the summit the wind got up and the clouds descended onto the top of the mountain. We could see no further than an arm's length in front of us and then the rain started. We took shelter behind a wall and I took the opportunity to discuss with the guys the joys of walking for three hours to get cold and wet and see nothing. I did go on a couple more of these trips and there was a satisfaction in reaching the top of a mountain but it was far better when you could see for miles and stay dry and warm.

It was during my time at Leuchars that the Stone of Scone (the Jock Rock) was returned to Edinburgh and RAF Leuchars was given the privilege of providing personnel for an honour guard for the ceremony. All sections on the unit were tasked with providing a set number of personnel to make up the guard and usually on such occasions a duty list is consulted to identify who are the next people in line to carry out such duties. However, on this occasion I decided that as this was such an auspicious occasion for the Scottish nation that only Scottish personnel would be used so as not to deprive them of playing a role in such a momentous part of their country's history. This decision obviously went down well with the English personnel in the armoury and the Scots could hardly complain!

It was around this time that the RAF introduced the GEMS scheme that rewarded personnel for coming up with ideas that would either improve efficiency, working practices or save money. All of a sudden, the guys and girls across the unit were hard at work thinking of GEMS submissions. In the early days of the scheme personnel got £25 just for submitting an idea (apparently it encouraged them to think) but the amount of ideas submitted became restrictive in deciding which were worthwhile and which were not. I was nominated as the chairman of the GEMS committee for the unit and very soon we had to adjust the criteria for the £25 award as people would put no thought or effort into the submission and were putting pen to paper just to get the money. There were, however, some fantastic submissions that saved thousands of pounds and others that had a huge effect on working practices.

One of the flight lieutenants at RAF Leeming had been told he was going to Cyprus for a month to support an armament practice camp (APC) and whilst he was happy to do so, he needed to come back for a week due to family reasons. He called me to discuss his options and I said I would cover the week for him but that I needed to clear it with OC Eng Wing prior to us making final arrangements. I went to see OC Eng Wing and explained the situation and highlighted that this was an excellent example of one Tornado F3 unit helping out another and that it is exactly how the F3 force should operate. He told me in no uncertain terms that he thought I was just after a holiday and that he would not let me go. I didn't get to go to Cyprus, alternative arrangements had to be made to support Leeming and the early trials of the whole force concept had fallen at the first hurdle.

I used my time at Leuchars to continue my NATO TACEVAL duties and managed to get away on a few TACEVALS as an evaluator. It was during this time that I had some of my more memorable TACEVAL experiences.

On an evaluation of a German Air Force base in northern Germany the EOD team was called out to an unexploded bomb on the edge of the technical accommodation site. After a long wait the EOD team arrived and started to assess the situation. After about an hour it was clear that the team were unsure what to do and decided to move their vehicle closer to the weapon to save them having to walk a long distance between the two. However, what they forgot to do was to maintain a safe cordon at the original location and a stream of traffic moved down the road with the team. Very soon there were around twenty vehicles in the danger zone as the EOD team continued to assess the situation. After a long wait the team tried to make the unexploded bomb safe by removing the fuze but were using the wrong type of tool. As a result, we determined that the bomb would have functioned as designed, killing not just the team but all the queuing personnel in their vehicles as well. It went down in folklore as the German Air Force trying to re-enact the road to Basrah from Gulf War One.

Later that year we travelled to south-east Turkey to carry out an evaluation on the Turkish Air Force. This trip was memorable for two reasons. Firstly, the evaluation was halted halfway through to enable the Turks to carry out a bombing raid on the Kurds as part of their long-running feud. It was quite bizarre as the whole of the NATO evaluation team were sent back to the accommodation for a day while the bombing raids were carried out and then the process carried on as normal.

Secondly, once the evaluation had restarted; and following a simulated air attack, a Turkish EOD team arrived to make safe an unexploded bomb. They sat at a safe distance and after about thirty minutes of inactivity we decided to go and see what was going on. The team explained to us what they would do and we instructed them to carry on as they would if the situation was real. They lifted a huge box out of the back of their vehicle, which was a remotely operated fuze removal tool, and told us that this was what they would use. We asked them to carry on. They opened the box and the tool was in kit form and looked like it had never been assembled. Again they explained what they would do but after being told again to carry on they got irate and started shouting and waving their arms around. It was clear at this stage that they had no idea how to assemble the tool in the box, never mind how to use it to carry out fuze extraction.

I also attended a TACEVAL in northern Norway in the peak of winter and while the TACEVAL itself was fairly uneventful it was a fantastic opportunity to visit Norway when it was knee deep in snow everywhere. One night as we travelled back from the Military HQ to the hotel we were passing by a large lake and all of a sudden, the sky began to shimmer and shine with a strange green glow. We pulled over to the side of the road to watch the amazing light show that nature was putting on for us. People pay a lot of money to go in search of the Northern Lights and often don't get to see them but here in front of us was that amazing spectacle. After a few minutes it faded and the sky returned to normal and we sat in awe of what we had just witnessed. We travelled the same route every night and were lucky enough to witness the Northern Lights one more time.

My two years were nearly over; manning were true to their word and my posting to the Falkland Islands came through. I explored the option with manning of going to the Falklands for twelve months accompanied rather than six months unaccompanied but was told that there were no married quarters available and that it was a non-starter. That being the case, I had decided that I would like a posting to 5131 (Bomb Disposal) Squadron on my return and asked for it to be confirmed before I left Leuchars. The plan being that Dawn and the kids would move from Leuchars during the summer holidays. Manning agreed to my request, I was to be posted to the Training Flight job on 5131 (BD) Squadron on my return from the Falkland Islands. I travelled to Brize Norton to catch the flight to Mount Pleasant Airfield (MPA).

Chapter 10

Falkland Islands

After sixteen hours of flying, interrupted by a two-hour stop in the cage at Ascension Island, the TriStar aircraft started its final approach to MPA, my home for the next six months. On arrival, it was like taking a step back in time with the very outdated air terminal and baggage carousel. As we received our arrival brief, telling us all of the dos and don'ts for the island, I caught a glimpse of a very happy-looking OC Arm Eng who was obviously elated that I had arrived to start the handover process. At that time, there were two flights a week from the UK to MPA, so the routine was that I would arrive on a flight, that flight would depart the following day and a couple of days later the next flight would arrive and that would be the one that my predecessor would depart on the following day.

After a very intensive four-day handover, it was time for the outgoing OC AEF to leave. We had one final check that all had been handed over, apart from the obligatory skeletons that would come out of the cupboard during the tour, and he boarded the aircraft, waving gleefully as he got to the top of the aircraft steps. It was a very foggy morning and as the TriStar thundered down the runway a large bang was heard just as it got airborne. One of the engines had suffered a major problem but the weather was too bad for it to get back into MPA so the aircraft diverted to Chile, were it was stuck for a few days until a replacement could be sent out with spares to replace the engine and recover the passengers. This type of incident was always a fear in the back of everybody's mind as it would delay your homecoming for anything up to a week.

The working routine on MPA was that of a five-and-a-half-day week with everybody working on Saturday morning. The background reason for this wasn't too clear but with nothing else to do at weekend nobody minded much. One train of thought was that it gave all section bosses the chance to make sure everybody had made it back after the Friday nights in the bars and gave the opportunity to have an end of week tidy up and FOD plod around every section.

The first job for anybody arriving in the armoury was to make a brass marker for the gozome board. The gozome board was a sequence of numbers on a board in the crew room that basically mapped your route home by counting off the days. The numbers went from 120 down to 0 for everybody in the armoury but there were additional numbers of 180 down to the 120 for OC Arm as it was a six-month tour as opposed to the four-month tour for everybody else. It was a World Cup year and as an avid football supporter I decided to make my marker a replica of the FIFA World Cup. Once I had cut out the shape, engraved the detail and attached the pin I placed it on the board in hole number 180, quite a soul-destroying act as it was going to take two months before my marker was in a place that had people coming on behind it.

The armoury crew room doubled as the Southern Comfort Bar, which was the armourers' bar. It was only open on a Friday night, or on special occasions, but every Friday was looked forward to by most of the members of the Arm Eng Flt and there was always good attendance and seldom any trouble. There were initiation ceremonies, rituals and speeches for all arriving and departing personnel as well as weekly awards for the good, the bad and the stupid.

It was all very well run with duty personnel to police goings on in the bar and duty drivers to make sure that everybody got back to their accommodation safely. In my six months there I attended the Southern Comfort Bar every Friday night except one and there were never any serious incidents. I returned on a staff visit some years later and the fun police had closed down the majority of the bars on camp, even those that were only open one night a week, and I believe that this eroded a great deal of the camaraderie and team spirit that was present during my tour.

It became clearer when I arrived as to why there was a shortage of married quarters that prevented me from doing a twelve-month accompanied tour. The NAAFI manager had a house, which was fair enough, but so did the deputy NAAFI manager, which was a bit strange. One of the MPA primary school teachers also had a married quarter. She was single and spent most of her time eating in the officers' mess dining room and drinking in the officers' mess bar; what a waste of a MQ that

I could have occupied with my wife and family. After a month or so OC Eng asked me to carry out a study and write a paper on making my post a twelve-month accompanied one. I pointed out to him that I had asked him to authorise that course of action a few months earlier and he had declined so could not see why the situation had changed. He told me to get on with it but I managed to handbag the task for the whole of my tour as a matter of principle and left it to my successor. The post did eventually change to a twelve-month accompanied one but even then, it was only when they could find somebody to fill it on that basis.

One of the key tasks for the EOD personnel in the armoury was to carry out crash site visits all over the island. These were sites that still had wreckage on them from the 1982 conflict and had a history of ammunition being found on regular visits. However, there were far too many still 'active' and it proved difficult to manage as most needed a helicopter to get to them. We decided to conduct a review of all sites, looking through records of historical visits to try to reduce the numbers to something more manageable. We decided that twelve sites would be the ideal number as it would only need one visit per month to carry out the annual visit requirement.

We made a concerted effort to carry out a full and comprehensive review and we achieved our aim by the end of my six-month tour. Visiting one site per month gave the EOD personnel in the armoury the chance to get out and about once a month, gain the experience of organising the visits with all the logistical challenges it brought, gave them the chance for a few helicopter flights and didn't put too much of a burden on the helicopter fleet. On the majority of visits, no ammunition was discovered but on one trip to West Falkland we found a BL755 cluster munition that had obviously been lying around since 1982.

On another occasion, we aimed to carry out visits to two sites that were relatively close together. The plan was to get dropped off at one site and after an hour or so get picked up and dropped off at the second site, where we would stay until the helicopter picked us up before returning to MPA later in the day.

A Chinook had been allocated to the task so we took the opportunity to take some additional personnel to give them the chance of a helicopter trip and to take a few people who rarely had the opportunity to get away from MPA. One such person was our squadron leader, who often questioned what we did on our trips and was always keen to understand the role of EOD operators. The first part of the trip went as planned; we transited to West Falkland and got dropped off at the first crash site. After an hour and a half, the helicopter returned, picked us all up and took us the twenty-five-minute flight to the second site with an agreement that they would return for us at about 1600. We checked the site, found nothing of interest and utilised our time on the ground to do bit of explosive handling training, which also served to get rid of the explosives. This made life easier during the transportation and was also easier for the explosive accountants as they seldom liked having opened boxes of explosives returned to the storage area and even less so after hours.

Well, 1600 hours came and went, as did 1700 hours, and no sign of the helicopter. Our radio expert started to set up the radio to make contact with MPA to find out what was happening. The radio expert demonstrated comprehensively that he was no longer a radio expert and wasn't sure how to set it up so we gave up on that idea pretty quickly. Since leaving MPA we had been snacking on our individual ration packs throughout the day and had very little food left and it was now starting to get dark. If we weren't picked up soon it was likely that we would be spending the night out here so we started to look for shelter and a place to set up our bivvi shelters for the night. We found a dried-up river bed that would give us adequate shelter from the wind and some of us started to make our bivvis. The overall mood was a mixture of disbelief and resignation but sprinkled with a huge dose of gallows humour that lightened the situation; well for some of us anyway.

All of a sudden, the unmistakable beat of rotor blades could be heard in the distance and we all scanned the horizon looking for the navigation lights of the helicopter. At the same time, we started to collapse our shelters and pack our bergens, and on looking across the landscape we witnessed a sight that will forever be etched in our memory. The squadron leader, in camouflage gear, against a background of grass and gorse and in failing light, was leaping up and down flapping his arms trying to attract the attention of the approaching helicopter. We pointed out that we could barely see him and therefore there was no chance of being seen from the helicopter. We set off a signal flare (brought for such occasions) and the helicopter headed in our direction. Then we noticed that the helicopter was a Sea King and not the huge Chinook that brought us out. The loadmaster managed to squeeze us all in and we set off for the return trip to MPA. It turned out that the Chinook had been retasked but the crew had forgotten to tell helicopter ops that we still needed picking up from West Falkland and it was a last-minute call from the armoury to helicopter ops that reminded them.

Prior to leaving RAF Leuchars I had enrolled on an Individual Self Studies (ISS) course as it was a prerequisite for promotion that was all to be done in your own time. What better opportunity to do this training than on a six-month unaccompanied tour in the Falkland Islands. It was all about how to write letters and what letters to write for particular situations. You would submit an item of work and it would come back covered in red pen markings, and that was fine, but you could resubmit the work and it would come back with recommendations to alter it back to what was originally there. It all seemed a fairly pointless waste of time but was obviously needed to keep lots of retired wing commanders in employment setting tasks and marking your work. I completed part one of the course while in MPA and would look to see about enrolling for part two when I returned to the UK.

As part of the upgrading of vehicles in MPA, the armoury received a brand-new Land Rover and it was designated as the officers' and SNCOs' vehicle for getting to and from work, travelling around East Falkland for meetings and visits, and was available for everybody to use for bimble trips at the weekend.

One Sunday the flight sergeant (FS) and I decided to go on an impromptu visit to Ajax Bay refrigeration plant. This was used as a hospital during the Falklands conflict and was the scene of some EOD heroism for which an RAF EOD operator received a Queen's Gallantry Medal (QGM). Nobody else wanted to go so the FS and I set off with our packed lunches and map of how to get there. The start of the journey was on gravel roads but this soon turned to mud tracks across the wilderness of East Falkland. We reached an inlet that needed to be crossed but it was dry so we made the crossing and after an hour or so reached Ajax Bay.

We had a look around and acquainted ourselves with the layout of the building and read through the history leaflets explaining the events of 1982. All very interesting and a great opportunity to relive that momentous occasion for RAF EOD. We took a few photographs of the buildings and the local penguin colony and then decided to set off back to MPA. As we approached the inlet that we had crossed on the way out it was apparent that the tide had now come in. We assessed our options and came up with two possible courses of action. We could sit tight and wait for the tide to go out or assess the situation and push on. After some discussion, and mainly due to the fact that that there was football on TV that we wanted to get back for, plus it was also going to get dark soon, we decided to try and push on. We walked down to inspect the route and depth and decided that it was probably worth going for it. I was driving and we entered the water making slow and steady progress. Then the water started to get deeper and deeper and the bow wave was getting bigger and bigger; it was just about to come over the bonnet as we started to climb and exited the inlet. We stopped to take a moment, breathed a sigh of relief and reflected on how we would have explained how OC Arm and FS Arm had lost the brand-new Land Rover, not to mention how we would have made contact with MPA or even managed to walk back.

Other than on my EOD course, this was my first experience of working closely with the Royal Engineers (REs). The Joint Service EOD organisation in the Falkland Islands consisted of the RAF elements who were based at MPA and the Royal Engineers, who were based in Stanley. In general, we had a good working relationship and had some very good joint training days and worked well together on the routine station exercises. However, they just had a different way of doing things. It was all about bluster and shouting, whereas we had a more measured and considered approach to everything. These traits could often result in clashes, as I would find out on numerous occasions throughout my career.

To set the scene; one such occasion resulted in a very long and drawn out task that created a lot of work for everybody involved. A few of the REs were on a social visit to Pebble Island and were exploring the wreckage of a crashed Argentinian aircraft from the 1982 conflict.

Early one evening, I got a call in my room to get my kit and meet at the helicopter HQ in twenty minutes, where I would be met by the Royal Engineer OC and a member of the Falkland Islands Police. We would be flying out to Pebble Island as a body had been discovered in a crashed aircraft by some REs. The Falklands Police had a very quiet life in general and decided to make this task its highest priority with all of the associated fuss that brings. We arrived at Pebble Island and were taken immediately to the crash site to be shown the body. It was a couple of bones very similar to what you would have left on your plate after Christmas dinner. The police declared the area as an investigation scene and after some discussion, during which I advised it was probably the remains of a dead sheep, the police decided that we would need to return at a later date to excavate the site, sweep the area, gather up the bones and anything else found before reporting on the incident and eventually closing the case.

This meant that the following week we would have to deploy RAF and RE EOD personnel, a JCB digger that had to be underslung on a Chinook helicopter, explosives and equipment to Pebble Island to carry out the task. In the meantime, I carried out some historical checks in the archives and discovered that the pilot's body had been recovered at the time of the crash. However, that did not deter the police from their high-priority investigation and the task went ahead. After a full day of excavation work we found a few more tiny bones and they were all packed into evidence bags to be sent back to the UK for DNA testing. We also found a few rounds of small arms ammunition, which we destroyed at the scene, and after carrying out a full sweep of the crash site area and the surrounding few hundred metres the site was declared clear and we all returned to MPA. The incident made the local newspaper and I suppose on an island where nothing much happens this was to be expected.

Several weeks later the DNA results confirmed that the bones were from a sheep! The moral of the story is that if you find something with legs, arms and a head it is probably a body; if you find a few tiny bones on an island inhabited by sheep then they are probably from a sheep.

The working relationship with the Royal Engineers was one of mutual respect coupled with the desire to get one over on each other if the situation arose. One such occasion was when walking around Stanley we noticed that the RE building on the seafront had a new sign that said 'Royal Engineers Explosive *Ordinance* Disposal'. A simple spelling mistake that was easy to make but a cardinal sin for anybody involved on Explosive Ordnance Disposal. We mentioned it to the RE commander when we saw him a few days later and he told us that the sign was indeed spelt correctly and that we must have been mistaken. They had changed the sign but unfortunately for them we had the foresight to get photographic evidence.

As we started to get towards the UK school summer holidays it was time for Dawn and the kids to move to RAF Wittering. The guy I was taking over from at Wittering had agreed to take over my married quarter at Wittering for me and hand the keys to Dawn when she arrived or leave them in the guardroom for her to pick up. She drove from her parents' house in Durham, with my parents in convoy, to Wittering to rendezvous with the removals people for a quick and easy move in. She went into the guardroom to register her car and get a station pass and asked if any MQ keys had been left for her to pick up. No keys in the guardroom. She managed to get the phone number of my predecessor and gave him a call. He sounded surprised to hear from her as he was not expecting anybody to call him that day as he had a few admin jobs to do but not much else. She asked him where he had left the keys for the MQ and at that moment the phone went silent; he had forgotten to take over the MQ. The removals men were chomping at the bit to unload and get away and were threatening to unload the vehicle in the middle of the street. With help from our new next-door neighbours they contacted the families' office and got the keys and managed to move in that evening.

During the holidays, the family managed to get an indulgence flight to the Falklands and we all stayed together in a Service Institute Fund (SIF) flat for part of the stay. However, they were unable to get onto the planned return flight and had to stay for another week. The SIF flat was already booked by somebody else so we had to use the transit rooms in the mess for the kids to stay in and Dawn stayed in my room. This was a great opportunity for the family as they got to see most of East Falkland, visited numerous battle sites and monuments, saw penguins in the wild and built snowmen in August. Dawn also got the chance to sample the delights and goings on of the Southern Comfort Bar on a Friday night.

The annual EOD dinner always took place at RAF Wittering late in the year and was always preceded by an EOD conference and briefings. Towards the end of my tour I saw this as an opportunity to try and get a week at home under the guise of attending the conference and dinner and this would give me the opportunity to get peace of mind seeing the family settled in at Wittering and recharge my batteries for the final few weeks of my six-month tour. OC Eng agreed to my proposed course of action with the plan being to fly back to the UK on the Wednesday, do the EOD conference (and the dinner) on the Friday and return to MPA on the Monday night. The TriStar arrived on time but was broken when it landed so a replacement had to be sent out.

It arrived on the Thursday and was due to return to the UK on the Friday; I might miss the conference but should still make the dinner if all went well. OC Eng said he was still happy for me to go but I still needed to be back on my original flight. My options were to either look at the same four walls of my room for another weekend or look at the inside of a TriStar; so I took the latter option as it least it would give me a break from the monotony of MPA. The TriStar was delayed and I eventually arrived back at Brize Norton at 10 o'clock on the Friday night where Dawn picked me up, but I had missed the dinner. After a weekend at home it was back to Brize Norton on Monday evening for the return flight. Sounds mad now but at the time it was worth it.

The sporting facilities at MPA were second to none and I spent the majority of my tour keeping fit by playing squash and five-a-side football. I also took the opportunity to play golf at both Stanley and Goose Green; both very different courses with their own different and unique challenges. The two characteristics they shared were the ferocious winds and the fact that they were both covered in sheep shit from the free-roaming flocks. Goose Green had several holes that were bordered by barbed wire fences with 'Danger Mines' signs on them, so searching for stray balls was not an option, and Stanley course was littered with shell and mortar craters from the conflict and these had over time filled with water. As a result, if your ball went in you weren't finding it and it you stepped in them they were often knee deep. Another way of keeping fit was to go out walking at the weekend. We did this on several occasions, the most memorable of which was when we set out from Mount Kent went over Two Sisters, up and over Tumbledown and into Stanley for a well-earned beer.

It was, as on previous units, the armoury task to arrange and carry out the annual bonfire and fireworks display. Not long after I arrived I had to start planning this as we had to order the fireworks from the UK and this had to be done in good time as they had to come out on the routine sailings. We ordered them and they arrived without any major issues. The station put together a working party to build the bonfire and everybody on the island saw it as the perfect opportunity to get rid of a lot of crap that was hanging around in the back of workplaces and married quarters. Therefore, the fire was huge and we used the tried and tested method of using incendiary devices to initiate it, but without the excess of fuel we had used at Wildenrath. We set up all of the fireworks and once the fire was lit and burning we set about carrying out the fireworks display. Thankfully all went off without a hitch other than the gale force winds, which made for an interesting evening dodging the fireworks and some very impressive photographs.

When the posting notice for my replacement arrived, it was not a name I recognised, which was unusual as I knew, or knew of, most of the EOD officers around the RAF. The TriStar landed and I went to the air terminal to meet him, such was the tradition, and I am sure I looked ecstatic as he caught my eye across the crowded lounge. I showed him to his accommodation let him settle in and then started our handover in earnest. Over idle chit-chat that evening in the mess bar I asked him when he had done his EOD course. 'I haven't done one,' he replied and added that when he questioned it in the UK when selected for the post, the manning desk officer said it was not necessary.

I saw my route home gradually closing in on me but we agreed to keep that little nugget of information our secret until the TriStar with me on it had taken off and was heading north. Eighteen hours later we arrived at Brize Norton and I travelled to Wittering to our MQ and my new job as OC Training Flight on 5131 (BD) Sqn.

Chapter 11

5131 (Bomb Disposal) Squadron (1)

I arrived at Wittering just in time to call in to see my new officer commanding at the squadron headquarters and my new place of work at North Luffenham before everybody broke up for the Christmas holidays. I had a much-needed few weeks off to get reacquainted with the family and then it was back to work.

I arrived at the Training Flight and was pleased to see several familiar faces as instructors and support staff on the flight. Once again, as a fairly experienced EOD operator with RAF Germany exercise and TACEVAL experience, getting to work was a fairly painless process. Additionally, having done the Airfield EOD (AEOD) course whilst in Germany I was familiar with the flight and airfield layout and the skills and knowledge associated with AEOD. In those days, we were training AEOD operators from all over the UK and Germany in AEOD, Combat Vehicle Reconnaissance (Tracked) (CVR (T)) driving and CVR (T) Gunnery. The workload was intense with six, six-week AEOD courses every year plus up to eight 30mm and general-purpose machine gun gunnery recertification courses. If you weren't delivering a course you were preparing for one starting imminently. The instructors were all experienced, professional and hardworking operators who thought nothing of putting in the extra hours to give students additional training to get them ready for the exams, the final test phase and the final exercise. The final exercise was carried out on the airfield at North Luffenham and started early in the morning with a set number of tasks having to be completed throughout the day by each team. It was routine for that day to go on till about 9 in the evening with the exceptional cases going on even later.

When I arrived the FS and the SNCOs were part-way through organising a range clearance exercise in the USA and had kept a slot for me if I was available. Needless to say, I was and they pressed on with the planning to take ten personnel from both the Operations Flight and the Training Flight on what would prove to be one of the most valuable training exercises ever experienced by RAF EOD operators.

We flew out to Las Vegas, had a couple of days off then drove down to 29 Palms in the Mojave Desert for five days of range clearance work with the United States Marine Corps. In that time we cleared numerous ranges, getting rid of all types of ordnance from 40mm grenades to mortars all the way up to 2,000lb bombs. We then drove back to Las Vegas and from there travelled daily up to Indian Springs to clear US Air Force ranges with the USAF EOD teams from Nellis AFB. Again this was an outstanding training opportunity, clearing a lot of heavy bombing ranges with 500lb, 1,000lb and 2,000lb bombs being disposed of.

However, the most valuable experience was clearing the cluster bomb ranges. We started with some ranges that hadn't been used for years and we were clearing cluster bomblets that we had only seen in books or in our recce circuit/museum at North Luffenham. Later in the week we went on to the more recently used lake bed ranges to clear the USA cluster munitions, predominantly the BLU-97. As the lake bed was littered with munitions, the USAF used a clearance process called 'Blow and Go'.

Everybody in the clearance party would line up at one end of the range, wearing helmet and body armour, and carrying numerous pyrotechnic time fuse-operated explosive charges. On the command, we would all start walking through the bomblet field placing charges next to any bomblet encountered and at the same time we initiated the time fuse, which had a ten-minute burning time. One person followed up behind to make sure we all stayed in a line and nobody dropped back too far. After ten minutes the first charges that we had placed started to detonate and we just kept walking and placing charges until we either ran out or we reached the end of the range. This was one of the most exhilarating experiences I have ever had and it really sharpened your senses and kept you on your toes. Once all the charges had gone off we walked back through the target area to check that everything had been destroyed and then moved on to another target. At the end of the week we returned to Wittering but little were any of us to know at the time that the training and experience we had just had would prove to be priceless over the coming months.

On returning to 5131 (BD) Squadron it became evident that the situation in the Balkans was getting worse and NATO forces had begun conducting intensive bombing raids against the Serbian forces in Kosovo. NATO was looking at options to drive the Serbs out and provide a stabilisation force to police and monitor the area and return life to normal as quickly as possible.

The MoD was looking at options for the UK commitment to this NATO effort and it was decided that an Army brigade would carry out this task as the lead element on Operation Agricola. Two key elements played a huge part in what became a defining moment for RAF EOD. Firstly, the Royal Engineers were struggling with EOD manpower and needed to bolster their numbers; secondly, because of the amount of air-dropped weapons used in the region it was considered necessary to have air-dropped weapons specialists on the ground; RAF EOD. Numerous meetings took place at the various HQs and I was asked by OC 5131 (BD) Squadron to represent the squadron's interests at a meeting at Carver Barracks, Wimbish, the home of 33 EOD Regiment Royal Engineers. It was decided in a very short space of time that the RAF would send four EOD teams of four personnel and an EOD commander to be embedded with 21 Field Squadron (EOD). This equated to around 33 per cent of the EOD manpower committed to the task, although the Royal Engineers did have a significant number of support staff to provide all of the real-life support to the squadron.

On returning to Wittering I debriefed the squadron commander and we started to look at options for nominating personnel for the operation. He started to talk to me as if I was going to be the EOD Commander and I pointed out that I had only just returned from a six-month unaccompanied tour in the Falkland Islands and that OC Operations Flight should be the one to go as it was an operations task. He said he saw my point but was sending me anyway as he had other things planned for OC Operations Flight. I was extremely aggrieved at this decision, as was my wife, especially as we had just put a deposit on a house that was due to be completed in July and it looked likely that the family would be moving whilst I was away again.

In hindsight, I am really pleased that I had the opportunity to do a front-line operational EOD tour of duty. We were inundated with volunteers to fill the sixteen positions needed but disappointingly a lot of the so-called EOD experts on the squadron were avoiding the issue and proving that whilst they could talk a good game they weren't prepared to take part. We would be deploying as four-man teams with each one operating from two vehicles (a CVR (T) and a Land Rover). A slightly different mode of operation for the teams but at least we were taking our armoured vehicles, which would prove invaluable during the first few months of the operation.

In parallel to all of this happening, the EOD Engineering Development and Investigation Team (EDIT) were carrying out trials in the USA and had been asked to look at disposal methods for Maverick missiles as they had been used extensively during the conflict. Not long before we deployed the EDIT sent back a procedure for getting rid of any unexploded Mavericks and had obviously been working very hard on the process as could be seen from the procedure they had written, 'Put the missile in a pit, cover it with plastic explosive and detonate'. Well, thanks for that highly technical procedure based on the US theory that, 'If it's not white it's not right'.

Personnel nominated, equipment and vehicles prepared, packed and despatched, the pace of preparation gathered and before long we travelled to various locations for briefings and training. We drove to Salisbury training area to carry out OPTAG (Operational Training Advisory Group) training but within hours of arriving there several of the Army operators were sent back to Wimbish to make the final preparations for deploying to Kosovo. We carried on and completed a very hurried and compressed training programme and made the dash back to Wittering to make our final preparations.

We completed our preparation and were given the call forward for the drive to Brize Norton to catch our flight to the operational theatre. However, first of all we had to endure the 'South Cerney Experience'. South Cerney was an airfield several miles away from Brize Norton that was used to gather people and baggage together and hold them prior to their flight to save them messing up the air terminal at Brize Norton. For us travelling from Cambridgeshire we drove past Brize Norton to South Cerney, where we handed our baggage over and sat around for hours waiting to be called forward for our flight. The facilities were awful, as was the food, and in true military waiting style everybody had built in a bit of extra time so that we wouldn't be late. This resulted in us leaving home some three hours earlier than we had to. Deep joy. After a lot of sitting around we were eventually called forward. We were transported by bus to Brize Norton and boarded the TriStar for our flight to the Balkans.

Chapter 12

Kosovo

After an uneventful four-hour flight we landed in Skopje in Macedonia while the aircraft dropped off some passengers and picked up some up others. The place was a hive of activity with UK and US transport planes bringing in load after load of equipment and personnel. We were travelling on to Thessaloniki in Greece, where we would meet up with our vehicles and equipment that had been shipped out and unloaded at the port. On arrival, we located our stuff and set off for the long drive north into Macedonia and the force rendezvous point at Petrovac training area on the outskirts of Skopje. Once at Petrovac training area all force elements were grouped into convoy packages and at the evening brief we were given our departure date and timings.

As an RAF officer in what was now a very Army-dominated environment (several thousand versus sixteen) I was not invited to the key briefings but was just given the 'essential information'; we would be leaving the following day. I woke up the following morning, having slept in a Land Rover, to find that several vehicles were missing from our convoy and was then told that the OC, the troop commanders and the sergeant major had all gone forward during the night for no other reason than that they obviously wanted to be the first into Kosovo. I had been excluded from the briefings, hadn't been given a map and was now in charge of our element of the convoy, which was due to move into Kosovo at sometime today. I managed to extract some more information, and a map, from the Brigade HQ elements and briefed the rest of the convoy members. It was soon time for our convoy to move off and we made our way towards Skopje and then to the border with Kosovo and into the Kacanik Defile. This was now real boy's own stuff and difficult to comprehend for all of us; RAF EOD vehicles driving into Kosovo with Chinook, Puma and Apache helicopters thudding through the skies above. Paras and Gurkhas guarded every bridge through the mountainous defile as we made our way north.

We were heading for our first port of call and overnight stop at a large factory complex at Uroševac and we were making good time. There is a saying in the military that implies you should never trust an officer with a map and the only thing worse than that is an RAF officer with a map. We passed what I now know to be Army tactical signs that should have guided us to our destination. However, this was another of the snippets of information that I had not been privy to and as we overtook some rather tired-looking tanks we noticed the Serbian flags flying from them. It turned out that we had overtaken the rear line of the retreating Serbian troops and were now leading them on their route north out of Kosovo. We soon realised our mistake, did a rapid U-turn and made it back to the factory at Uroševac. That night we kept radio watch in our vehicles and the following morning continued north towards our final destination of Pristina.

The drive north was memorable for numerous reasons, especially for a group of RAF armourers who could never have anticipated where life would take them in June 1999. Many of the buildings in the small villages were still burning from where the Serbian Army had tried to drive people from their homes and reap a final act of revenge before the NATO forces arrived.

There were numerous examples of mocked up wood and plastic bridges and tanks that had obviously been used as deception targets during the air campaign. As we arrived on the outskirts of Pristina we were told to make our way west to a VW garage and to set about making that our home.

After several days, we had stripped the garage bare, got rid of all of the rubbish and started to make the building a secure and comfortable home, which would become even more so as the weeks and months went on. As with most garages, the VW site had flagpoles outside and we used these to fly the RAF ensign that we had brought with us. This caused a little bit of angst amongst our Army colleagues but they soon produced their ensign and the Joint Service EOD HQ was now truly established.

The Army were less understanding with the 'Royal Air Force Bomb Disposal' signs and badges that we had on the side of our armoured vehicles, and the sergeant major instructed the guys to paint then over. They objected to this request and we all got into a very heated debate about the reasons for it and the merits of carrying it out. There was no give or take and, in the end, we agreed to cover them with tape. The sergeant major agreed with our course of action. We covered them with tape and took it off every time we drove out the camp gates.

Tents were pitched around the main garage building, a cook house was built and furnished with wooden chairs and tables and the quarter master (QM) was very quick at getting contracts set up for portable toilets as the one long drop toilet in the garage was heavily overutilised. Contracts in those early days are always problematic to establish and we initially only got one chemical toilet for use by the whole unit, which at that time was getting on for being seventy-strong. Coupled with the extreme heat of the Balkans summer the toilets could be smelled from many yards away and there was always a race for the toilet when it got its daily cleaning as it was the only time it was going to smell half decent.

We quickly established an HQ with radio communications installed and as tasks were already coming in from the dispersed regiments we set about compiling a task register to keep a check on what tasks had been reported and which had been completed. As every unit was establishing their domestic and working accommodation they were finding items of ordnance, or suspected ordnance, both large and small and work would always stop until the item had been removed or destroyed. On the majority of occasions the items were often innocuous pieces of scrap metal but in the early days of conflicts such as this it was better to be safe than sorry.

The EOD teams were often out at first light, not returning till dusk as they covered the miles, ticking off tasks at an alarming rate. Most of the teams would complete between six and eight tasks per day with some finishing even more if the tasks were close together or quick to resolve. In the first twenty days we completed around 500 tasks.

This theatre of operations was defined, from an EOD perspective, as one that would be dominated by cluster munitions. Most of the nations involved in the air campaign had used such bombs and the country was literally covered in them.

The failure rates of cluster munitions were historically around 10 per cent for most types but in the heavily wooded areas where the munitions had a softer landing that failure rate could often be as high as 60 per cent, which left a great deal of unexploded bomblets to be disposed of with cluster bombs carry anything between 100 to 200 individual munitions. This is where our training on the US ranges a couple of months earlier paid dividends, as did the deployment of our armoured vehicles. We were familiar and confident in dealing with most types of cluster munitions and keeping control of every disposal operation was made far easier by operating under the cover of armour well inside the danger area.

In the first couple of days of the clear up campaign a couple of Gurkha engineers were killed during an operation to clear cluster munitions from a school house. Along with some Kosovo Liberation Army (KLA) soldiers, they were moving cluster munitions out of a school house to a safe patch of ground for future disposal. None of them were EOD qualified or familiar with the types of munition and as somebody had already moved them into the school house once they determined that they were safe to move again. One of the KLA soldiers tripped and fell whilst carrying numerous bomblets and they detonated as he hit the floor, killing two KLA soldiers and two Gurkha engineers. The first EOD team on scene at this incident included some RAF EOD personnel who were helicoptered in to clear up the aftermath.

We would often turn up in villages to find people coming out to meet us holding cluster bomblets and asking us to get rid of them. We would always stop and try to educate the locals on the danger of picking up these bomblets and often found that the best way to do this was to get the village elders to gather everybody together whilst we demonstrated what happens if the bomblets explode by exploding one in a controlled environment.

That method generally got the message across but there were still times when we would fence off an area covered in bomblets and erect warning signs to come back and dispose of the bomblets at a later date. On a few occasions, we did this and then that evening would get a call to say some locals had been killed wandering into the area. When we went back out to the area concerned we found that they had removed the fencing to use it for other purposes, leaving the area unprotected. A sad but real fact of life.

I was soon moved into the Brigade HQ as the Staff Officer (SO) for EOD as the previous incumbent had to return to the UK. I quickly settled into the task and really enjoyed running an EOD HQ that was controlling the tasking of all UK EOD teams. At this stage, we had hundreds of outstanding tasks registered and it was clear that it would take a Herculean effort to complete them all, but we would do our best.

The first evening in the HQ my radio operator asked me what time we were going to do the radio transmission that detailed the new tasks reported that day and the tasks completed.

Apparently, this transmission was done every night at the same time so that all Regimental HQs could listen and take note. The event was affectionately known as 'Radio Verity', named after my predecessor in the SO3 post who instigated the task. I suggested that we did not do the broadcast and see how many people complained about its absence. As I suspected, nobody complained or cared and sixty minutes of air time was freed up from that evening onwards.

For the duration of the operation, Kosovo was divided into five sectors, with each one being given over to a nation as their area of responsibility (AOR). The primary nations responsible for each AOR were the UK, USA, Italy, France and Germany, with many other countries contributing to the effort.

In the build-up to the NATO push into Kosovo, the Russians had made a dash from the north and taken control of Pristina airfield. A small RAF Force Protection HQ was allowed onto the airfield by the Russians as the negotiating team due to it being in the UK AOR. This negotiating team was dealing on a daily basis to secure access to the airfield as it was vital to the humanitarian effort to bring in supplies. Eventually, it was agreed that RAF Pristina would be established alongside the Russian contingent and that RAF EOD teams would be permitted on to the base to commence clearance operations as it had been heavily targeted during the air campaign. Once again, it was a historic time for RAF EOD as we were using armoured vehicles to clear a liberated airfield, which was our modus operandi that we had trained for for many years and now we were doing it for real for the first time.

The sights around the airfield were jaw-dropping to say the least, with huge bomb craters on the aircraft operating surfaces, but the runway was largely intact. Several of the taxiways had the remains of aircraft on them and often this included partly burnt out air-to-air missiles that needed to be destroyed. The terminal was being used as the Russian HQ and the basement needed to be cleared as it would eventually have to be reverted to a baggage and cargo handling facility. However, this was flooded and the Russians had been using it as an open toilet but nobody would start to clear it out until it had been declared clear of unexploded ordnance. It was a very unpleasant task for the RAF EOD teams wading around in a flooded basement that had all manner of detritus floating on top.

The Tactical Communications Wing turned up with some despatch rider motorcycles that they used for quickly transporting equipment and data between sites. I had just passed my motorcycle test before deploying and managed to borrow one of their bikes for an afternoon. I used it to carry out a full recce of the runway and surrounding areas; another first for RAF EOD; airfield recce on a motorbike.

One day, as we were clearing some outbuildings around the main air terminal, we discovered a small haversack that was suspiciously hanging on the back of a door. After cordoning off the area we reported to the Russian Ops centre what we had found and asked them to check with all of their personnel that the haversack did not belong to any of them.

After twenty minutes the Russians confirmed that it did not belong to any of their personnel so we set about devising a plan to safely move and remove or destroy the item. This task was made more difficult as we did not have any remote-controlled bomb disposal robots with us and the Royal Logistics Corps (RLC) who had that equipment had not yet arrived in theatre.

We developed a plan and a procedure, and were just beginning to set about the execution of the task when a Russian soldier walked through the cordon up to the building, picked up the haversack and walked away. It had belonged to him all along and he had obviously not been asked during the initial confirmation phase seeking to find out to whom it belonged. This incident did little to boost our confidence in working closely with the Russians.

On the subject of robot availability, we had several incidents in the early days of booby traps being set to frighten or injure local community leaders. The favourite method was to simply tape instantaneously fuzed hand grenades to fences or trees and tape a piece of string connected to the grenade pin to door handles. As the door was opened the pin was pulled from the grenade and it would detonate instantly, spreading fragmentation in all directions. At best, it would frighten the individual but at worst it would severely injure or kill them. These incidents were fairly easy to disarm or destroy but were never without risk of injury to the EOD teams.

After a short time, the Russians identified a large area of land that they decided would be ideal for establishing RAF Pristina so we set about clearing it at the earliest opportunity. After a couple of days, we declared the area clear and as the FP HQ started making plans for establishing the base they were told that the Russian commander had changed his mind and had identified a new area for the RAF. After a great deal of debate, we were given the task of clearing the newly identified area and it came as no surprise as we witnessed the Russians establishing their permanent base on the area that we had recently declared clear.

The new area was going to be far more difficult to clear as it had obviously been subjected to cluster bomb attacks during the air campaign and was littered with unexploded bomblets. They were literally everywhere; on roofs, in buildings but most worrying were the ones in the long-grassed area that would need to be completely cleared. Metal detectors did not work as there was so much scrap metal lying around, so the only way to clear the area was to walk line abreast, mark the bomblets and then dispose of them. The grass was knee deep in many places and on numerous occasions we would walk back in to check the area of an explosion to find more bomblets uncovered as the grass had been burnt off by the explosion. At one stage, we became so concerned with the number of bomblets we were finding that we looked at different ways of clearing the grass area. We even tried setting light to small areas at a time to see if we could burn off the grass, exposing the bomblets or even setting them off. I had inadvertently started fires on several EOD ranges in the past but for some reason this grass would not burn and we ended up reverting to walking the line. We were all very well-trained operators, vigilant and meticulous but as with all EOD work there is always that element of luck and not standing on these bomblets as we walked in and out of the area was extremely fortunate.

Once the area was clear, the FP HQ started to call forward the RAF contingent that were waiting in Macedonia. I was asked to fly to Macedonia to brief the incoming FP HQ and contingent elements on what to expect when they arrived at RAF Pristina. I will always remember this moment as flying out of an operational theatre to let the RAF Regiment know that it was safe for them to enter! RAF Pristina was quickly established and we stayed on site until all areas that were needed for infrastructure building, etc, were declared clear and after that we went back to our VW garage home on the outskirts of the city but remained on call to return if needed.

When OC 21 Field Squadron (EOD) went on R&R he decided that, as I was the most experienced operator amongst the officers, I would stand in for him whilst he was away. This again was another outstanding opportunity for me and one that I dined out on for the remainder of my time in the RAF. There can't be many RAF officers who can come up with phrases at joint service meetings such as, 'Well when I was OC 21 Field Squadron it was never like that.'

This two-week period gave me the opportunity to get out and about around the key work areas for the squadron and sample all the different aspects of the EOD work that we were doing, as opposed to sitting in the HQ and just tasking teams out to them.

On one occasion I went to the meeting with all the non-government organisations (NGOs) that were working in Kosovo doing various tasks. They were working alongside the UN and the key task was deemed to be clearing schools to allow them to start up again and teach the children. I was given a list of schools for us to clear and we all had to report back with progress the following week.

At the next meeting, each of the NGOs stood up and declared their achievements for the week. The majority declared, quite proudly, they had cleared two or three schools, with some doing slightly fewer and some slightly more.

It was my turn. 'This week we have cleared thirty-seven schools.' (We actually completed those tasks in two days.) Everybody looked at me in disbelief but the figures and details were there for all to see. My theory on this is as follows: The military were getting paid as normal and liked being busy so therefore were working balls out to clear as much as possible. The NGOs on the other hand were getting paid by the day or hour, so if you did it fast you spent less time on task in total and therefore got paid less. Some NGOs would find safe areas but pretend they were dangerous and spent days clearing them but more often than not found nothing of any significance.

The high-priority clearance of schools was of vital importance to the UNHCR as they needed to get the schools operating as quickly as possible. However, we did have cause for concern regarding the accuracy of their reporting. We were sent to clear a couple of schools about two hours north of Pristina and on arrival all we found were two concrete pads with no walls. It was obvious that these buildings had not been recently demolished and the UNHCR had just taken somebody's word that the buildings actually existed; a complete waste of a day.

It was also during my time as OC 21 Field Squadron (EOD) that the Engineer in Chief (Army) (EinC(A)) visited both the Brigade HQ and the sites of some of our more interesting tasks. One task in particular springs to mind and that was the assistance we were giving to the International Crimes Tribunal Yugoslavia (ICTY). They had started to gather evidence on war crimes that had taken place during the Serbian occupation and the most harrowing of tasks was the exhumation of bodies from mass graves. Reports from witnesses indicated that people had been shot and thrown into trenches that had then been filled with earth, but more sinister were the reports that hand grenades and mines may have been thrown into the trenches under or with the bodies.

Because of this risk we were asked to devise a method of checking for ordnance as part of the exhumation process. We developed a procedure in quick time and it worked OK but was tweaked during each use to make it more efficient and safer. All of the teams took it in turns to do a week at a time working on the mass grave sites with the ICTY but it was a truly harrowing task made worse by the pungent smell of rotten flesh in the summer heat of the Balkans.

It was suggested that EinC(A) would like to visit one of the sites to see the work being done and as OC 21 Field Squadron I would meet him on site and talk him through the process. As a show of the truly joint service nature of the operation, we would have both RAF and RE teams on site. We demonstrated the process to the visiting party and I explained how we did the metal detecting and ordnance removal process but did not handle any human remains. As I was explaining this the ICTY investigators were lifting a heavily decomposed body into a tin bath for removal and transportation. All of a sudden, the Army team leader, wearing rubber gloves, started to sift through the remains explaining how he was looking for bullets and what he would do if he found any. The accompanying Army photographer was enthralled and started taking photographs and telling us all how the pictures would look great in *Soldier* magazine (or the RE equivalent). I had to stop them both from doing what they were doing and apologised to EinC(A) for what he had just witnessed. Once the brigadier had left the area, the team leader was rebriefed on the procedure and the photographer was ordered to delete all photographs.

Throughout my time in Kosovo we completed hundreds of tasks and the work rate remained high throughout those early months. Whilst it would be impossible to recall all of the tasks carried out, I have outlined in this chapter some of the more memorable tasks. They were memorable for a variety of reason from the funny to the dangerous and from the stupid to the serious but mainly because of the multinational nature of them. At the height of the clearance tasks we had around twenty different nations operating in our AOR.

One such tasks was nicknamed 'the Italian Job' as it was carried out in the Italian AOR. The Italians had EOD teams on the ground but claimed to be unfamiliar with the unexploded bomb they had discovered on the outskirts of a town. We agreed to assist and carried out a planning visit to make final arrangements.

It was clear from the beginning that the Italians were very wary of the task in hand mainly because of the close proximity of some houses. They stated that they would notify all people in the danger area and set up a safe location with tea and coffee for all occupants who had to be evacuated, and all we had to do was get rid of the bomb. On the day in question we travelled to the area and met the Italian Army, who confirmed that all residents had been evacuated and we set about preparing the task of attempting to deflagrate the bomb (making it explode but with far less power than a full detonation). We used service-supplied equipment and water suppression barriers to minimise the impact on the nearby houses. The Italians were very dubious that our methods would work and at the last minute tried to call off the task. We reminded them that the Operation Order they wrote put us in charge of the disposal task and we carried on.

At the published time of the explosion being initiated the button was pressed, a subdued bang came from inside the barriers and they stayed perfectly in place. The team leader went forward to inspect and discovered a perfectly split open bomb that was now safe to remove and transport to a safe location to be fully destroyed. A perfect task execution that had the Italians amazed.

One of the RAF teams had come back from a 500lb bomb task with a souvenir of the complete baseplate from the bomb of which they had disposed. One of the Army teams had a similar task planned for the following week and asked how the RAF team had achieved their goal as they wanted a souvenir baseplate for their HQ back in the UK. The RAF team briefed them on exactly what to do and off they went to carry out the task. Several hours later they returned looking extremely sheepish, dejected and with no souvenir. When we asked what they had done they stated that they thought they should use two charges instead of one as they had heard about someone doing that the previous week. When they initiated the charges, the bomb detonated and there was nothing left to recover, just a large smoking hole in the ground. We pointed out that we had told them exactly what to do and that the team the previous week had used two charges because it was a larger bomb. Sometimes there is just no telling people.

The Royal Engineers always used to train all their personnel in EOD even if it was not their primary task. This often meant two things; valuable places were taken up on heavily oversubscribed courses by people who would rarely carry out EOD, and by rarely carrying out EOD these people seldom became proficient.

One fine example of this was when the field squadron QM decided on a quiet day that he would take out his own QM and support team to carry out an EOD task. They drove to an area where a large bomb entry hole had been reported and they set about trying to locate the bomb. After several attempts at probing the hole for the bomb they thought they could feel it and started to excavate the ground to gain access. Having failed to carry out the routine procedure of identifying any underground services, they hit a water main, flooded the area and deprived some local villages of a water supply for a few days until it was repaired. Not the greatest way to win over the hearts and minds of the local population.

Another example was that one Sunday afternoon in the Brigade HQ we received a radio message from the squadron sergeant major asking for a task number and details as he was going out on a drive around the local area and wanted to carry out a task. I called the squadron HQ to get details on what the situation was with this strange request and the squadron OC told me it was OK and instructed me to provide the task number. Alarm bells started ringing and I questioned again as to who was in the team. I was informed that the team consisted of the sergeant major, the chief clerk and a driver, and on hearing this I stated that I was unhappy with the constitution of the team and was not prepared to send them out on an EOD task. The OC reaffirmed that he was happy and instructed me to issue a task number. I asked the OC to give me an instruction in writing to issue the task number to this badly constituted and partly untrained team, so that if anything went wrong my arse was covered. At that point, he agreed that letting them go out on an EOD task was probably not the best idea. He explained to the sergeant major the reasons and off they went on a drive around the local area.

Once the RAF Regiment field squadron turned up we went on patrols with them in the hills above Pristina airfield. For them, it was to identify key advantage and defence points for the airfield, and for us it was to identify any unexploded ordnance and subsequently destroy it if needed. There was a fuel storage depot on the hill side that had obviously been subjected to a precision-bombing attack during the conflict as each fuel storage tank was destroyed but there was no collateral damage.

On the other side of the ridge was a large ammunition storage area that had also been subjected to a precision-bombing attack and as well as every building having been hit and destroyed it had also scattered the building contents far and wide. There were cluster munitions, aircraft ammunition, small arms ammunition and air-to-air missiles spread as far as the eye could see. We spent the next few days working our way through the area destroying all the ammunition and ordnance that we found.

On one occasion, we found a cluster bomb that had been badly damaged in the bombing raid and decided to cover it in plastic explosive and destroy it where it lay. We notified all personnel in the area and on the airfield below that we would be carrying out some controlled explosions to get rid of the ordnance. As we detonated the plastic explosive we noticed an intense plume of flame coming from underneath the cluster bomb and watched in disbelief as what must have been an air-to-air missile buried underneath the cluster bomb burned ferociously. Fortunately, the missile must have been pointing into the ground as it stayed where it was as it burned out and did not fly uncontrolled into the distance.

Explosive ordnance recognition (EOR) is key in post-conflict zones as everybody is on edge not knowing what is dangerous and what is not. It is in situations like this that you rely on the knowledge and experience of certain elements of the military to make life easier and you would hope that infantry units would be good at recognising ammunition, mines and mortars. However, the Parachute Regiment were responsible for patrolling Pristina and they called in a suspicious item they had found on the street. They described it as a possible mortar, 8 to 12in long with four fins. It sounded very feasible and potentially dangerous, especially as it had been found on one of the busy streets in the city. The area had been cordoned off with some buildings evacuated and roads closed. We sent the quick response team to the rendezvous point, where they met the incident commander and the person who had reported the item. After a bit of detailed questioning, some drawing of diagrams and discussing safe routes in and out of the area, the team leader made the long and lonely walk towards the potentially lethal piece of ordnance. He discovered a large lead fishing weight about 5in long with four hooks at one end; potentially dangerous to a fish but not to the general population of Pristina. We recovered it to the Brigade HQ and used it to design a poster reminding people of the importance of good and accurate EOR. I made a few minor alterations to the poster and displayed it behind my desk in the HQ. This was at the time of the Army recruitment advert that had the catchphrase 'Army Soldier, Be the Best'. My poster read 'EOR, Be the Best'. It lasted a couple of days before I was told to remove it; the truth hurts I suppose.

The Russian EOD teams found a half-buried bomb on the hillside above Pristina airfield and notified Kosovo Force (KFOR) HQ that they would be attempting to render it safe the following week and would be putting a 1-mile exclusion zone around the location. KFOR HQ were a bit suspicious of the Russian techniques and procedures and asked me if there was any way we could keep an eye on them from a safe distance. Once again this was a perfect opportunity to use the RAF armoured vehicles for the purpose they were employed in by the RAF EOD organisation. We moved into the exclusion zone and monitored proceedings from about 400 yards and observed everything that the Russians did. The task went off smoothly with no problems and we remained safe and secure under the cover of our armoured vehicles.

One of the RAF teams was tasked to a row of mines that had been placed across an access road in one of the local villages. On arrival, they saw what looked like a lot of small anti-personnel mines that had been placed in two rows across the road. The team leader decided to lay some detonating cord around the mines and detonate from a safe distance. He prepared the cord and initiating charges and walked towards the mines to lay them down. On arrival at the mines they turned out to be tins of vegetables. Somebody had obviously decided to do this either to cause a nuisance or to check out the operating procedures for our EOD teams. The team leader decided to carry on as planned and laid his charges, returned to his armoured vehicle and pressed the detonating button. A loud bang was followed by lots of vegetables all over the road and the area was declared safe.

We were asked by KFOR HQ to clear an area of land in a fairly innocuous location and when we questioned the reason for this we were told that another nation's EOD teams were coming into our AOR but their ability was not known. We were to clear the area before the other nation was tasked with clearing it. This enabled the other nation to carry out a task that was 100 per cent safe as it had been cleared by the UK EOD teams first. It gave them the opportunity to feel involved and gave KFOR HQ the peace of mind when tasking them.

On a similar vein, we were contacted by both the Norwegian and Belgian EOD teams as they moved into the area and began to establish their HQs. They each asked us to clear some 500lb bombs that were in their AOR. We asked why they did not carry out the task as they were qualified EOD personnel but they wanted us to do it. We offered them advice and assistance but stopped short of doing the task for them.

The Swedish EOD platoon moved into the area and identified a building that they would be using for their HQ and base. They called us and asked for us to provide them with a clearance certificate for the building as we had quickly passed through it a few weeks earlier. We had a rather heated debate with us explaining that we had only quickly passed through the building at the time and we were certainly not in the business of giving clearance certificates to EOD organisations as it was their job to do the clearance. After a lot of to-ing and fro-ing between us and getting KFOR HQ involved it was agreed that EOD organisations should be doing their own clearance work and issuing certificates if needed.

The Finnish EOD teams turned up and came straight to us for advice and assistance, which was fine as we had been here the longest. However, it soon materialised that they were after some maps of the area as they had deployed without any. There were also reports from KFOR HQ that there were EOD teams in our AOR from Poland, Hungary and the Czech Republic but we never came across them and they never asked us in the Brigade HQ for any of our outstanding task numbers or details.

We got a call to send a team out to a communications site a few miles west of Pristina as somebody had reported seeing a large bomb lying next to one of the buildings. When we arrived, it was obvious that the site had been subjected to a heavy bombardment during the air campaign. There were several buildings on the site and each one had been completely destroyed and all that remained were the walls and a lot of rubble and destroyed technical equipment.

We located the unexploded bomb that had been reported and decided to do a thorough check around the area prior to carrying out a render safe procedure. On searching around, we found two more 500lb bombs and an entry hole that seemed to go on forever. One of the 500lb bombs was standing on its base plate and looked like it was looking out of the window. Because of the number of bombs on the site we cordoned it off and decided to come back another day and carry out a planned operation and dispose of all three bombs at once, as well as trying to see if we could locate anything in the entry hole.

A few days later we returned to the site, destroyed the three 500lb bombs first and then set about investigating what was in the hole. After a few hours of digging we had still found nothing and decided to leave it alone. If there was anything there it would take a huge force to make it detonate and it was so far underground that it would have little impact on anything going on at the surface.

Another task with a similar outcome to this was the report of an entry hole next to a disused petrol station on the outskirts of a town called Komorane, west of Pristina. When we turned up you could see a large hole in the petrol station roof and then following the track of the hole you could work out where it had slammed into the garage forecourt and kept on going. We knew that this would be the likely scenario and had taken some heavy-duty excavation equipment with us. We probed the hole and found nothing in the first 2m so started to excavate and after a couple of hours we had a hole that was 2m deep and about 4m wide on the garage forecourt. We probed the bomb track hole again and found it kept going for at least another 2m, so we continued excavating until we reached the edge of the main road. By now we were more than 3m down, the bomb entry hole showed no sign of stopping and we had a difficult decision to make; do we backfill the hole and leave whatever was there or do we close the main (and only) road while we continue to excavate. In consultation with the HQs the decision was taken to backfill and leave as the risk was low, balanced against the prolonged closure of a key transport route.

Another interesting task we had was when we discovered a type of cluster bomblet that we had not previously encountered either in Kosovo or during any of the training we had taken part in. We managed to contact the USA EOD teams in the neighbouring sector and asked them for advice on what it did, how it worked and how we should dispose of it. The US team said that they could not give us the information but would travel to our AOR and get rid of the items for us. We stated that we needed the information as we could not keep calling them back if we found more, but once again they refused. We then pointed out that either the US EOD team should give us the information we needed or we would exploit the item we had found to find out what it was and how it worked. They said we could not do this but were quickly reminded that we could do whatever we wanted with ordnance found in our AOR. Reluctantly they admitted that we held all the cards in this particular exchange of views and they agreed to give us the information we wanted.

Throughout our time in Kosovo our service identity was very important to us and never before, or since, in my time in the RAF have I witnessed all ranks wearing their berets at all times as it was the only piece of uniform that signified that you were a member of the RAF and not the

Army. It was shortly after this operation that additions were brought out to the RAF combat uniform such as 'Royal Air Force' patches, coloured tactical patches and coloured stable belts, and I would like to think that we played a part in the introduction of those additions.

This pride in our service coupled with the constant animosity between the RAF and the Army led to some hilarious incidents as the pace of tasking slowed down and people had a bit more time to do the fun things. The best example of this was when one of the RAF teams acquired a 4ft tall inflatable alien and named him 'Sapper'. The Royal Engineers were overjoyed that the RAF had decided to call their alien mascot after them and were very supportive when photograph requests were made.

The truth was that the inflatable alien was full of hot air and had nothing between his ears, and that is why he was called Sapper. Sapper was posed and photographed all over the operational theatre in places such as portable toilets, the gym and even the hospital operating theatre, to mention but a few.

In the September it was coming up to the annual Battle of Britain celebrations and some of the RAF officers in the recently deployed Logistics (Logs) Brigade suggested having a Battle of Britain parade outside the Brigade HQ. Unfortunately, there were no junior ranks in the Logs Brigade and I mentioned to the FS what had been suggested. He was all for it and rallied the guys together on the day in question. We managed to get a sizeable RAF contingent together and paraded outside the HQ. We synchronised our parade timing with the one at RAF Pristina and by doing so were able to share the helicopter flypast. An incredibly moving moment for the small RAF contingent in this Army-dominated theatre of operations.

I mentioned earlier in this chapter the KLA, who eventually agreed to be disbanded or downgraded and became known as the Former KLA. This all seemed very innocent until it developed that they preferred their title to be referred to in their native tongue where the KLA was the UCK and so the Former UCK was born. But for some reason the abbreviation was seldom used on posters or correspondence.

In the later stages of my four-month tour I got a call from the ISS team at Bracknell telling me that my ISS part 2 assessment was due in (I had passed part one whilst in the Falkland Islands). I informed them that I was on an operational tour in the Balkans and that, as I was working on average fifteen hours a day, seven days a week, I would not have the time to complete the module. They informed me that my excuse was not good enough and that they would be reporting me to my commanding officer. Sure enough I had a call from my boss a few days later, who understood my stance but was only ticking the boxes as the team had complained to him. We discussed my options, which were fairly limited at the time, but in the end agreed that now was not the time to complete ISS.

It was another stunning example, and confirmation if I needed it, of how some ageing and retired senior officers whose only role in life was to put red pen on service writing work had no concept at all of life in the modern RAF.

After three months it was obvious that the pace of life was slowing down dramatically and all the relevant HQs started to look at how to draw down the number of troops in theatre. As is often the case, the Army needed us at the start but were keen to get rid of us at the earliest opportunity and keep the operation to themselves. However, we fought long and hard to keep a foothold in the operation as it was a good operational tick in the box for the RAF operators and ensured that we stayed relevant in an ever changing and competing world. We managed to get an agreement that we would retain one team but lost the opportunity to have any of the command and control positions. Right across Kosovo the effort was to try and demilitarise as much as possible, so the armoured vehicles were returned to the UK and all EOD teams adopted more peaceful stances and way of operating. A new RAF team was sent out at the four-month point and the four original teams and I returned to RAF Wittering.

Chapter 13

5131 (Bomb Disposal) Squadron (2)

After arriving back at Wittering, we all took some well-earned leave and returned to work to find that a medal ceremony had been organised for all the returning personnel and their families. As a team, we had been awarded a commendation by the Commander-in-Chief of Strike Command and the Air Officer Commanding was presenting all medals and the commendation at the ceremony. It was extremely pleasing to be honoured in this way and it meant a lot to me and the rest of the team. We had been the through a lot of heartache in an Army-dominated environment but had come through it with flying colours and had earned the respect of not only our own chain of command but also of the Army as a whole.

Very soon it was back to work as normal. OC Operations had had a nice summer holiday whilst OC Training was doing operations and, in my absence, it had also been decided that OC Training would now become OC Training and Support. This would allow OC Operations to concentrate on all operations (except for operations) and would leave me to do everything else, including having people working for me who were 14 miles away next to OC Operations. Sounds mad and it was.

We now, for the first time, had operationally experienced EOD operators on the squadron and, more importantly, as instructors on the Training Flight. We set about amending training packages and adjusting training courses to reflect reality but without losing our core values and niche capability of the armoured EOD clearance of airfields.

Shortly after we all returned to work back at North Luffenham, a trial had been arranged to check the containment properties of the box body section of the soon-to-be-introduced Wedgewood bomb disposal van. A new box body section had been purchased by the scientists and they turned up in large numbers to record and document the process of detonating an explosive charge inside the van. The experiment would serve two purposes, one would be to check the containment properties of the internal containers and the other to check the containment properties of the box body section itself.

Our role was to provide a safe range and to supply and detonate the explosives. Once everything was set up the scientists retired to the HQ building and range control to record and observe the events. 'Stand-by, firing, now.' A huge explosion and the box body was converted instantly to matchwood, but the good news was that the other explosive items in the vehicle had remained intact. As we declared the area safe and returned to the HQ building we were all looking forward to the slow-motion replays from the remote filming that had been carried out. As we sat looking at the monitor the blank screen became the focus of attention. No replay, no footage, the scientists had forgotten to turn the camera on! There was no second attempt to be had as there had only been one box body purchased for the trial, which although successful was a little bit weak on video evidence.

For some years 5131 (BD) Squadron had been taking part in an exercise called Phoenix Readiness, which was a USAF mobility exercise that took place at Fort Dix in New Jersey. I had heard great stories about this exercise and decided it was time to get myself on it at the earliest opportunity. We looked for a convenient gap in the training programme and a party of ten personnel from the squadron went on the next one.

We flew from Heathrow to Newark airport, picked up the hire cars and drove into New York for a couple of days' stay before driving to Fort Dix. We were able to do this as we stayed in the Soldier, Sailors, Marines, Coast Guard and Airmen's Hostel right in the middle of New York City. A very grand-looking building from the outside but inside it was a very different story with bare floorboards, bunk beds and tin lockers, with one shower and one toilet per floor. The key thing for us was that it was cheap (only a few dollars per night) and in a prime location just around the corner from the Empire State Building. We had a weekend of military tourism seeing how many of the New York sights we could tick off in our couple of days there and in fairness we did pretty well, visiting most of the key attractions.

On the Sunday evening we drove the three hours to Fort Dix and checked into our accommodation ready for the pre-exercise training to

A portrait of the author prior to starting his last role in the RAF as OC 5001 Squadron. (*Crown Copyright*)

The author photographed by his parents after his basic training passing out parade at RAF Swinderby in October 1977.

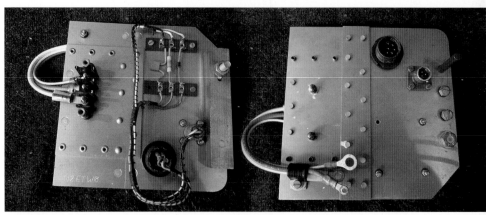

The final test job. The culmination of weeks of basic engineering training at RAF Halton, showcasing all of the mechanical and electrical skills taught to Weapons Technicians at the time.

The personnel of 16 Squadron photographed at RAF Laarbruch in 1982/83. The author can be seen in the back row, eighth from the left.

Buccaneers and the support Hercules getting ready to leave RAF Goose Bay in Canada for the next leg of the journey to Exercise RED FLAG at Nellis Air Force Base in Nevada, USA.

Aircrew and groundcrew of both nations pose for a photograph during a squadron exchange with the Danish Air Force in Karup. The author is sitting on the wing, fifth from the right.

A selection of patches from the early stages of the authors' career. Many of the groundcrew had their overalls plastered with patches in the 1980s.

The authors' 'pride and joy' – a tax-free Ford Escort XR3 bought during his first tour in Germany at RAF Laarbruch.

The nuclear deterrent. An example of the WE177 bomb that the author loaded to 16 Squadron Buccaneers during his time at RAF Laarbruch.

The author standing in front of the Berlin Wall during a tour of East and West Berlin whilst on the RAF Germany Corporals' Course.

A Buccaneer in 16 Squadron colours.

One of the appearances by the authors' name on the infamous Deci Wall at RAF Decimomannu in Sardinia.

A Hunter T7 in the colours of 208 Squadron.

An example of the Bomb Disposal armband worn by all Bomb Disposal operators before the badge was introduced for wearing on uniform.

'All smiles', the author having graduated from Initial Officer Training at Royal Air Force College Cranwell.

A humorous photograph taken of 8 Flight, 160 Initial Officer Training Course 1996. The author is wearing his beloved West Ham United shirt. (*Kamara Photography, Lincoln*)

A misspelt sign on the Royal Engineer Ops Centre in Stanley, Falkland Islands. The sign was changed a few days later, though the author and his colleagues already had photographic evidence.

The Falklands Islands plaque presented to all Weapons personnel on completion of their 4- or 6-month tour.

The author suited and booted prior to carrying out 'Blow and Go' bomblet clearance on ranges in Nevada.

The RAF and British Army convoy at Petrovac Training Area in Macedonia waiting for the call forward to move into Kosovo at the start of Operation AGRICOLA.

A convoy of Serbian tanks retreating from Kosovo, pictured after the author and his unit had overtaken it!

RAF Bomb Disposal vehicles ready to start the clearance of the airfield at Pristina having been given permission to do so by the Russians.

A framed display depicting the author's time in Kosovo. Operational T-shirt designed for the RAF teams; RAF, Royal Engineer and RLC badges plus the Brigade badges and security pass.

'The Kosovo Team' – the RAF contingent during Operation AGRICOLA.

Surveying the scene of an unexploded 400kg bomb on the ranges in Oman during Exercise Saif Sareea II.

A model of RAF Bomb Disposal armoured vehicle presented to the author when he left the EOD Training Flight.

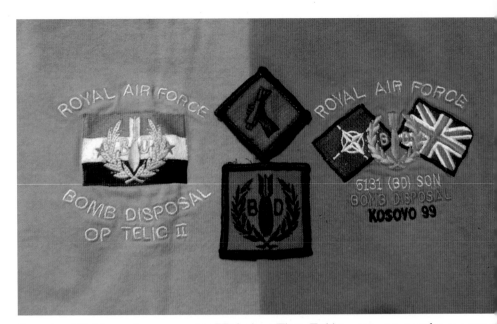

Operational T-shirts and accompanying BD badges. These T-shirts were very popular as a way display single service identity in an Army dominated environment.

The author enjoying the weather and a bit of down time during Exercise Flying Fish on Tioman Island, Malaysia.

The limited issue, personalised, commemorative RAF BD 75th anniversary watch.

The 5131 (BD) Squadron 75th anniversary commemorative coin.

The authors' career in a picture
frame. Medals, airman's and officer's
cap badges, first and last rank, stable
belt and, of course, the BD badge.

start the following day. Over the first few days we did familiarisation training on US explosives and EOD tools, driving Humvees and using US weapons. Later in the week we did MOUT training (Military Operation Urban Terrain) using laser weapons so that you could see who was getting shot and who was not (a bit like Laser Quest but on a much larger scale).

Every time one particular RAF SNCO stood up, his laser warning initiated immediately and nobody could understand why. The US operators could not work out what the problem was and even after changing batteries and sensors and giving him a new set of equipment it still kept happening. Then everybody heard sniggering from the undergrowth and one of the SACs was sat there shooting him every time he stood up. We all saw the funny side, apart from the SNCO in question.

Towards the end of the week we all had the chance to do abseiling from a huge wooden tower in the woods and then we progressed on to fast roping. With abseiling, you always have a safety man who can stop your descent by pulling on the belay rope but with fast roping there is no such luxury. The only thing stopping you thumping into the ground are your own hands and feet as you grip the rope to control your descent. Everybody had to do three successful fast rope descents to be signed off and have the opportunity to fast rope from a helicopter on the first day of the actual exercise.

Historically the helicopter seldom turned up as it belonged to the Air National Guard and was often tasked to do other things. However, on the Saturday morning we were informed that the helicopter had been confirmed and that we would be fast roping into the exercise area the following morning. Now we were all extremely nervous as we had all just assumed that it was not going to be available. We checked that everybody still wanted to do it and a little bit of gentle peer pressure meant that it was unlikely that anyone would drop out.

The following morning we stood on the edge of a large field in the training area with our equipment and fast ropes. The tension increased as the dull thud of helicopter blades could be heard in the distance. A massive Sea Stallion helicopter appeared over the trees, landed in front of us and the loadmaster signalled to us to move on to it. We all filed in and sat looking at each other as the helicopter lifted off and did a circuit of the training area. The loadmaster lifted the panel out of the centre of the helicopter floor, attached the fast rope to the suspension frame, dropped the rope down the hole and summoned us all to sit in a line behind each other and prepare to fast rope on to the training area. There was no turning back now as, one by one, we made the 100ft descent and after the last person was out the rope was released and the helicopter did another circuit.

It came back around and landed again and we were summoned back on to the aircraft for another fast rope descent. We did three in total and once again this was a thoroughly exhilarating experience that very few people got to take part in, especially a bunch of RAF armourers. The rest of the exercise went smoothly and we attended the end of exercise presentation and then packed our stuff away and drove back to New York for a couple of nights before flying back to the UK.

To summarise this experience: we had a couple of weekends in New York, drove Humvees, blew things up, had laser shooting practice and fast roped out of a helicopter with some US Army Rangers. Wow!

A few months later I had the opportunity to attend another Phoenix Readiness course with a completely different group of people. The USAF instructors had appreciated my input on the previous visit so much that they gave me the honour of joining the black cap cadre, which was effectively an instructor, and directing staff for the exercise.

The course had altered slightly on the second visit but it was fundamentally the same format with all the same modules running up to exercise week, however this time we were not lucky enough to get a helicopter to fast rope from. The best moments for this course were more from the recreational side of the experience, with two things standing out from the rest. One was a night playing pool in Kelly's Bar in Wrightstown, when it turned out to be one of those nights where everything was going right. I was partnering another RAF operator and we just kept winning and no matter what we did or who we played it seemed like we could not lose. We started playing at around 9 o'clock and by 11 we were unbeaten. A couple of people came in who wanted to play singles and not doubles, so my partner stepped aside and let me play and they were seen off quickly.

One person came in with their own cue and chalk and started to do lots of stretching exercises prior to taking me on. My partner and me looked at each other and thought that our winning streak was about to end. The challenger made a fantastic break but was unlucky that none of the balls went down; I stepped up and cleared the table in one visit and they were very upset and skulked back out of the bar. We went back to playing doubles and decided that once we got beaten we would retire to our accommodation as we had an early start the following day.

At 3 am we ran out of challengers and retired. The following day we were really struggling to stay awake and at lunchtime somebody took a photograph of both of us fast asleep in our car. Needless to say, the photograph did the rounds back in the UK.

On the weekend visit to New York it was the first time for most of the guys so they set off on the usual tourist box-ticking exercise. A couple of us decided that we would do some of the other sites, including the UN Headquarters and the World Trade Center. Little did we know as we stood on top of one of the twin towers that they would not be there six months later following the events of 9/11.

The RAF EOD reputation as a competent and current EOD operator was growing and as a result we received a request from the Royal Navy to support one of their exercises that was taking place the following summer.

It was called Exercise Flying Fish and would be taking place in Malaysia. While the Navy had their niche capability of clearance diving sorted out they wanted to refresh their operators on air-dropped weapons and to do that they needed a specialist. Due to a variety of different reasons, it turned out that I was one of the few who were available and willing to take part in the exercise.

First of all, I needed to convince the squadron boss that he should let me go and set about a strategy of introducing the existence of the exercise into our regular weekly meetings. I then started to talk about me going on the exercise and received no resistance, so just kept on feeding the information in small doses. The boss and I went to a meeting at the MoD and afterwards we went for a sandwich and a coffee and he started asking me about the exercise. We talked as if I was going, so I took that as read and put my name forward to the Navy.

It all went as planned and soon it was time to deploy on Exercise Flying Fish. I met with the Navy Fleet Diving Unit (FDU) 2 at RAF Lyneham, where we would be loading all of our equipment on to the

Hercules aircraft and flying out the following day. That night we got a call from flight ops saying that the aircraft was unserviceable and we would be delayed by at least twenty-four hours. Not a good start or a great place to be for the only RAF guy with twenty-five Navy divers as 'Crab Air' failed again.

We eventually got away the following day and after a night stop in Cyprus headed for the next overnight stop at Salalah in Oman. We checked into our hotel for the night and soon after got a call from the Hercules crew telling us that the aircraft was unserviceable again and we would have to wait at least forty-eight hours for spares. There are worse places to be stuck than in a nice hotel in Oman but it still did nothing to endear me to my Navy colleagues. The spares arrived after three days and we set off on the next leg to Sri Lanka, where we would be meeting up with all the other delayed elements of the trail, of which there were many as the RAF had several combat and support aircraft taking part in the exercise.

After two nights in Sri Lanka everybody gathered at Colombo airport for the final flying leg to Singapore.

There was a VC10 tanker in the trail and I won back some brownie points when I bagged us all seats on it for that final leg. It was quieter, more comfortable, we had space to spread out and the icing on the cake was the chance to watch Tornados air-to-air refuelling as we crossed the Indian Ocean.

On arrival in Singapore we had missed the multi-national Navy fleet, which had already sailed towards their final destination of Tioman Island off the east coast of Malaysia. The British Embassy had chartered an old fishing vessel for our party to travel to the island, so we spent the next ten hours bobbing around in the sea crammed into an ageing and very uncomfortable fishing boat that made the Hercules seem like business-class travel.

We eventually arrived at Tioman Island. It was literally a paradise island that on its west coast had a five-star hotel complex and on the east coast was our less palatial, but some would say more exotic, accommodation. There were several rows of small wooden huts (or chalets) with basic beds and a shower. We were just down the beach from where they filmed *South Pacific*. It was a very basic but beautiful holiday complex where people from the five-star resort would come to experience Malaysian island life the way it used to be. As we were the last to arrive we had a lot of hard work ahead of us to unpack our equipment and set up our camp area in a very short space of time. Once established we had a very nice, if somewhat primitive, camp area that was only a short walk in one direction to a beach bar and in the other direction to a beachside cafe and convenience shop. There were huge monitor lizards roaming freely around the site and every evening at dusk small bats started flying frantically around the accommodation area and high up in the tree canopy huge fruit bats would set off on their search for food. The showers in the huts were at best basic and getting wet often involved chasing the trickle of water around the shower cubicle. However, every day at about 3 pm there was a huge tropical thunderstorm and with the warm temperatures and high humidity this proved to be the best opportunity to get a decent wash. To the outsiders it must have looked like some strange ritual as we all covered ourselves in shower gel and stood out in the tropical downpour to get showered.

The other nations had been there a few days already and were well established but they all chipped in and helped us get set up. We now had a self-contained detachment consisting of Navy divers from the UK, Australia, New Zealand, Malaysia and Singapore – and one UK RAF officer. Each nation took it in turns to develop clearance diving scenarios for the other nations to tackle and I developed air-dropped weapon and land service ordnance scenarios for all diving units to attempt.

As well as carrying out scenarios on the land, we also developed ship-borne scenarios, and these proved to be very interesting and successful. It gave me the opportunity to fly out to different nations' ships in their helicopters to set up and monitor the scenarios, which again was an excellent experience that few people get to have.

The most interesting of these trips were the Blackhawk helicopter trip onto an Australian frigate and a Lynx trip on to HMS *Newcastle*. Whilst on *Newcastle* we were in a convoy of ships that were firing their guns at artillery targets on a neighbouring island. I was invited onto the bridge as *Newcastle* pounded the targets with devastating force, an experience I will never forget.

On one of the down days we decided to go to the five-star holiday complex to sample the delights. There were two ways to get there; one was to hike for a few hours over the mountain through the jungle and the other, preferred, option was to take one of the rigid inflatable boats and sail around, which took about an hour. A few people did attempt the walking route but due to badly signposted tracks and failing light a few of them did not make it back all the way and decided to sleep in the jungle overnight. They made it back just before breakfast looking decidedly weary and worse for wear. It turned out that lying on the damp jungle floor, with animals screeching all night and bugs everywhere, is not conducive to a good night's sleep.

Two weeks quickly passed by and after what had been a hugely successful exercise it was time to pack up and start the recovery operation. We were due to sail back to Singapore on a Singapore Navy support ship but we were having a night stop in the five-star hotel first. We sailed around to the hotel and checked in for a luxury night's stay. I had got my training shoes wet on the way round and put them on the window sill of my room to dry out. When I woke up the next morning one of my training shoes was missing and after enquiring at reception they told me that items should not be left outside as they would likely be taken by the monkeys that roamed the area. I went back to my room and had a look around and out of my window. There on the telephone lines strung between the telegraph poles was a large monkey with a luminous green training shoe in his mouth. I waited and kept checking around the area but he never dropped it or returned it.

After breakfast, we set off in the inflatables to the waiting Singapore Navy ship for the overnight passage back to Singapore. The ship was an old Second World War US Navy vessel that they had sold to the Singapore Navy for $1 rather than scrap it. It was slightly better than the trawler that had taken us out to the island two weeks earlier, but only just.

We arrived in Singapore docks and as all the nations bade farewell to one another the New Zealand Navy divers treat us all to a superb rendition of the Haka. Goodbyes completed, we went for an overnight stay in a Singapore hotel prior to flying out the following day. That evening we got a call telling us that the Hercules aircraft scheduled to take us back to the UK was unserviceable and that we should stay in the hotel until advised of our revised travel plan. Unlike on the trip out, nobody seemed too bothered that we were stuck in Singapore and we all took the opportunity to see the sights and make the best of our time there. We visited Changi prison, Sentosa Island and, of course, went for a Singapore Sling or two in Raffles Hotel. After four days we were asked to report to the airfield to look at recovery options and I went along with the Navy WO and chief petty officer (CPO) to see what we could arrange.

It turned out that a TriStar was due in a few days later to recover the air component of the exercise and it had sufficient spare seats to recover the Navy component as well. We booked ourselves onto that flight and went back to our hotel for a few more nights in Singapore before making the homeward journey without any delays or hitches.

Back on 5131 (BD) Squadron the new OC Operations Flight passed the EOD course but then had to have some time off work so it was decided that I should takeover Operations Flight until a new OC could be posted in.

I was now OC Training & Support Flight and OC Operations Flight and was spending a couple of days a week at Wittering and three days a week at North Luffenham; all manageable but extremely frantic at times.

In the meantime, a new squadron boss was posted in and he decided to do his Airfield EOD course to sharpen up on his skills and drills and get to know the members of the Training Flight.

During one of the lessons on bomblet clearance he questioned the disposal methods being taught by one of the instructors. We were teaching a USAF-modified version of the procedure that was used on USAF ranges to completely eliminate any risk of personnel being injured by shrapnel. The boss and OC EDIT had conferred between them and decided that what we were teaching was wrong and summoned me to a meeting to discuss the issue. OC EDIT was adamant that we should be carrying out the procedure in a different way to that being taught as he deemed that it was scientifically impossible for anything to go wrong, sending shrapnel in the teams' direction, and therefore we should do it by the book using UK-published procedures.

The instructors and I explained that if you were clearing munitions on a USAF range, as we had on many occasions, you would have to do it our way and that is why we were teaching it in such a way. I asked OC

EDIT how he had carried out the procedure when he was in the USA and he explained that he had done it the way we were teaching it and at this point I was struggling to see what his issue was other than it being an opportunity to gain some brownie points at my expense.

On the final exercise and assessment phase of the course the squadron boss had a bomblet clearance task to carry out and opted to do the procedure by the book and not the way we had taught him. After a prolonged period of analysis and having laid his explosive charges, the boss decided to move his vehicle to a different location. When I asked why he had opted to do this he explained that it was just in case some shrapnel came in his direction. I reminded him of the discussion we had earlier in the week when he and OC EDIT pointed out that it was scientifically impossible for that to happen and therefore he should stick to his beliefs and carry on as normal. He gave a sheepish wry smile and accepted that he may have been a bit hasty with his analysis and criticism of the Training Flight and its instructors.

We received a request from the Royal Australian Air Force (RAAF) for several of their EOD teams to attend the Airfield EOD course as they were planning to set up a similar training establishment in Australia and wanted to gain some knowledge and experience. The request was agreed by us and the MoD and a few months later we ran a course specifically for the RAAF operators. It was a huge success and all the Training Flight members got a huge amount of satisfaction delivering the course. The RAAF operators were superb and we all made some good contacts that would prove to be valuable in the years to come.

There was a large squadron push to participate in Exercise Saif Sarrea 2, which was a large, multi-force, exercise taking place at Thumrait in Oman. This exercise was being organised and run like an operation and therefore we all had to endure the 'South Cerney Experience', which for some was a first encounter but for others, me included, it was a dreaded revisit.

We arrived in Thumrait just as the exercise campsite was being completed and to say it was austere was an understatement. It was a camp established to house somewhere in the region of 1,500 people and we were living in non-air conditioned twelve-man tents with portable toilets and solar shower bags. The temperature was in the region of 35 degrees C.

The mobile catering people had set up a large dining facility and as usual the food they produced was fantastic.

We had two bombing ranges to look after for the duration of the exercise: Aqzeel Range, which was about an hour's drive from Thumrait so it was easy to do as a day trip, and RAS Range, which was about a five-hour drive north and required the team to drive up and stay there for a few days at a time in even harsher conditions with no toilets or catering facilities.

The day trips to Aqzeel were always interesting and even driving up there just to do some training was better than hanging round at Thumrait. Before our first trip we got together and briefed all of the teams on convoy discipline and the hazards that would be encountered on the journey as the roads were not tarmac and were covered in loose stones. After we set off we got so far and one of the Land Rovers in our convoy came speeding past us! We got to the range and once we sorted out our admin I took the renegade team leader to one side and asked him what he thought he was playing at as we had agreed that we would not be overtaking. He stated that he understood the plan but he had forgotten to brief his driver. On the way back the same thing happened again and at that stage he was read the riot act and told that if he stepped out of line again he would be confined to camp at Thumrait for the rest of the exercise.

On the first bombing run onto Aqzeel range the aircraft dropped four 1,000lb bombs at the same time from low level and all four failed to detonate, with them bouncing along the target area for several hundred metres. With four unexploded 1,000lb bombs on the range, the Omanis closed it and that was it for flying for the day. We drove out to the target area and found three of the bombs very quickly (we found the fourth one the following day as it had bounced for nearly half a mile) and set about making a plan to get rid of them.

None of the three team leaders had ever dealt with a real unexploded bomb before and here they were getting the opportunity to do one each on the first day of the bombing phase of the exercise. We prepared the charges with time fuse initiation and placed them next to each of the bombs. Once we were all set the team leaders ignited the time fuse and we climbed into our vehicles to retreat a safe distance. One of the vehicles got stuck in the sand after only a few yards and we all frantically tried, successfully, to dig it out. We reached the safe area with a couple of minutes to spare and observed the three bombs detonating from a distance.

On another day, the aircraft were going to be doing laser-guided bombing and as we sat around the range buildings waiting for events to begin we heard the sound of vehicle engines outside. We looked outside and saw a dozen bearded warriors starting to unpack their vehicles. I asked what they were doing and they replied that they were here to drop bombs. I pointed out that they needed aircraft to achieve that feat and that I didn't think Toyota Land Cruisers would be man enough for the task. They didn't see the funny side, told us where to get off and carried on unpacking their vehicles. After thirty minutes or so they decided that they wanted to be on the other side of the range to carry out the laser designation task for the aircraft and started to pack their vehicles, having identified a ridge that they wanted to drive to. I pointed out that they should drive around the range to the ridge as we were expecting a bombing run soon, but they ignored me and set off across the centre of the range to their new vantage point. Just as they cleared the target area two Omani Air Force Jaguars thundered through the mountains and dropped two 400kg bombs.

The following week we already had a team up at RAS Range and it was time to swap the personnel over as they had been there a few days. As we packed the vehicles in the evening ready for an early start the following morning we heard on the news that the US had commenced offensive operations against the Taliban in Afghanistan. Everybody was unsure as to whether the exercise would continue as normal and, more importantly, if we should still be travelling deep into the Omani desert. After a quick chat with the security experts it was decided that we would carry on as normal and the following morning we set of for RAS Range.

On arrival we met with the team who had been there for the past three days and as the range was due to be busy that day we decided we would all take part in the activity and they would travel back the following day. As mentioned earlier, it was pretty much as austere as you can get from a living point of view: a single 12ft × 12ft tent in the middle of a vast desert, solar shower bags hung from the back of the Land Rover for washing and a shovel to dig a new toilet every time you wanted to go. There were no catering facilities, it was twenty-four-hour ration packs for the duration of the visit and as much bottled water as you could transport up to the range.

We went out onto the range as flying was about to start and within minutes we had our first UXB. The aircraft were dropping laser-guided bombs from 20,000ft plus and you could barely hear them as they approached the target area.

We travelled out to where the UXB should have been and found it straight away. It had hit a rock formation and as it forced its way into the rock all the explosive had been squeezed out like toothpaste from a tube. We gathered it all up and destroyed it.

As we were tidying up the remains we got a call from range control saying that the next aircraft was overhead and seeking clearance to drop its bomb. We stated that it would take us fifteen minutes to clear the target area and that the aircraft should hold off until we were clear but the Omani controller wanted to let them drop their bomb immediately and told us to drive faster. After a heated discussion, we managed to get the aircraft to hold off and when he did drop the next bomb it detonated as planned.

Later that day we moved to another range target as some Omani Air Force Hawk aircraft were due to drop some 400kg bombs on a flat sand bed target. We parked off to the east of the target as the aircraft would be travelling north to south and sat and waited for the action to commence. Out of the blue we got a call from range control stating that the aircraft would now be approaching the target from east to west and that we should be on the lookout for the aircraft coming from behind our location. The Omani forward air controller who was with us seemed unfazed by the instruction but we were a bit more nervous and asked for them to either revert to the original north to south attack pattern or give us twenty minutes to move location before the bombing started.

We tried to tell the Omani forward controller that he should be the one determining attack direction on the range and not the pilots but he seemed reluctant to go back and tell them to either change or hold. In the end, we took control of the situation and got the aircraft to revert to the north to south attack pattern. After the four aircraft had passed and left the range we drove to the target expecting to see six craters from the bombs that had exploded and two unexploded bombs. When we reached the target, there was nothing there so we scouted the area and found the bombs and craters about 700 yards short of the target area; if they had been allowed to use the east to west attack run they would have bombed us.

A few of the guys on the team had a penchant for naked EOD and carried out the demolition of the UXBs wearing nothing but boots, a floppy hat and a utility belt.

The following day we doing some range admin tasks and whilst clearing up some target-marking barrels we saw a dangerous-looking snake. One of the Omani soldiers who was with us took out his pistol, cocked it and started to shoot. He wasn't a very good shot and after emptying his magazine had only succeeded in making the snake very angry and slightly wounded. We decided that the best way to remedy the situation was to prepare an explosive charge and clear the snake that way. Needless to say it worked a treat, even if it was a bit of overkill.

Towards the end of the initial exercise phase we were subjected to some classic Army-style punishment. There was a bar on camp that had a strict two cans of beer a night rule. It had been working perfectly well for weeks until some Army chaps decided to drink more and then urinate on somebody's tent and equipment. Rather than punish the individual, who had been caught red-handed, the Army commander decided to close the bar; one idiot steps out of line and 1,000 sensible people get punished.

The CSE show (entertainment for the troops) was scheduled to come out to Thumrait and a lot of people were getting very excited as Gerry Halliwell was the headline act. Once again, the whole event was being organised by the Army, so what could possibly go wrong. A stage and arena were erected out in the desert and everybody had to apply for places at the show. It was on the same night as England's crucial World Cup qualifier against Greece so a lot of people, me included, chose to stay at Thumrait and watch the football. However, those that were successful in bidding for places at the CSE show were bussed to the arena with their crates of beer and shepherded into a holding compound to socialise before the main event. With little notice, everybody was informed that they would soon be moving to the stage arena but no alcohol was allowed and they had to either drink it or leave it in the desert. Needless to say, nobody wanted to leave their beer so they drank it as fast as they could. Just imagine; hot weather and dehydrated people drinking lots of beer as quickly as they could and try to guess the outcome. Yes, you got it, rowdy people, violence, lots of vomiting. Well done Army.

As we were starting to pack up at the end of the exercise phase a few of the team were staying on to do some demonstrations but the rest of us started to pack our stuff away. The renegade SNCO from earlier in the exercise turned up wearing a full Omani Air Force uniform and claimed that the detachment WO had told him that it would be OK for him to travel back dressed like an Omani. I told him it would not and that he should go and get changed but he looked at me in disbelief and told me that what he was wearing was all had as he had swapped it for his RAF uniform. After another meaningful discussion, he had to go and beg, steal and borrow enough RAF uniform to travel back in.

The pace of operations in Afghanistan was ramping up and 5131 (BD) Squadron were putting a case forward for them to be involved. It was agreed that if there was to be an air component presence at Kabul then 5131 (BD) Squadron would provide the EOD support for that component and the airfield.

In parallel to this happening the squadron boss was trying to sort out postings in and out for the flight commanders and out of the blue I got a call from the manning people asking me if I wanted a posting to Wyton to work in the Sidewinder missile project team. The thought of working at Wyton looking after an ageing and soon to be out of service missile did little for me, so I declined the offer only to be told that if I did not accept it I would be posted somewhere else as the squadron boss was keen to move me on and get some new blood in. I was offered an ultimatum of either taking the Sidewinder job or going to RAF Cottesmore as OC Eng Co-ord and Plans (EC&P). At another defining moment in the history of RAF EOD, 5131 (BD) Squadron were deploying to Afghanistan and I was going to look after budget spreadsheets at Cottesmore!

Chapter 14

Cottesmore

This is likely to be the shortest chapter in the book, and possibly one of the shortest in any book, but here goes.

I arrived at RAF Cottesmore to take up my new post as OC Eng Co-ord & Plans Flight (OC EC&P) or OC Egg, Chips and Peas as it was affectionately known around the RAF. This would be my first ever non-armament tour and I decided before I went to Cottesmore that I would give it a good go because, after all, the job allowed me to continue living at home, it was something new to learn and being the aircraft fleet manager for the Harrier Force would be a very challenging, high pressure and high-profile job.

My optimism didn't last long as on my arrival chat with OC Eng Ops Squadron he informed me that the Harrier fleet management task was carried out by the WO and I would primarily be involved in flight commander duties for the flight, and more importantly I would be the Eng Wing budget manager.

He then went on to explain that his working routine was that he came in at just before 8 am, gave himself a fairly generous lunch break (he lived in married quarters on base) and worked through until 6 pm; the implication was that I should be doing the same.

I explained that if it was OK with him I would also start just before 8 but would not have a lunch break and would go home at 5. He seemed a little taken back by my declaration but was OK with it.

The posting to Cottesmore literally turned out to be the job from hell unless you loved spreadsheets and budgets, but as an ex-armourer and weapons-experienced branch officer it seemed like a complete waste of my time and experience.

All I did was compile spreadsheets from the other Eng & Supply Wing flight commanders, reconcile them with OC Eng Wing and then send them to the station budget manager for her agreement. Once that process was done it was time to start on the following month's round of spreadsheets and so on. Taking the minutes at the monthly fleet management meetings was about as close as I got to any aircraft engineering.

I began the process of trying to identify how an engineering aircraft fleet management job had been turned into this budgeting spreadsheet job and it materialised that my predecessor was into budgets and spreadsheets and saw this as a great opportunity.

I set about trying to revert the job to what it should have been and identified the requirement for OC Eng Wing to have a budget manager and started to set the wheels in motion to establish a civilian post to carry out the task.

After about a year in the post the Gulf War kicked off and again RAF EOD was going to play a huge part in the operation, deploying teams and personnel to five different countries in preparation for the entry into Iraq. The EOD Role Office, based at Marham, had sent personnel to man some of the command posts in the Middle East and were looking to replace those personnel with experienced EOD operators to man the support task for the impending conflict. I sensed an opportunity to escape from Cottesmore and get back to doing something meaningful, so made some enquiries with the EOD Role Office and the manning people to explore the options. Hallelujah! After only fourteen months at Cottesmore I was posted to the EOD Role Office at Marham. Result!

Chapter 15

Explosive Ordnance Disposal (EOD)
Role Office Marham

The EOD Policy Office was the part of the EOD Role Office that I worked in. It was affectionately (I think) known as 'Lunn Policy', which was a play on words relating to a holiday firm that was around at the time called Lunn Poly. By the end of this chapter you will understand why.

The daily drive to RAF Marham wasn't great but at least I was back doing something worthwhile and that was made even more so as Gulf War Two was now in full swing. RAF EOD had multiple teams deployed to various locations in Saudi Arabia, Kuwait, Qatar, Jordan and Cyprus all waiting for the move into Iraq.

We were in constant contact with the deployed teams through the chain of command and were receiving almost daily requests for additional equipment. Once the initial entry into Iraq was complete the pace slowed down significantly, which allowed the teams and the HQ to consolidate.

During my time in the Role Office a lot of my time was spent on the road travelling to EOD equipment meetings at various locations around the UK, but most of them took place in the south-west of England at Abbey Wood, Andover or Salisbury.

I was due to travel to Abbey Wood one day and was scheduled to have an overnight stop as the meeting was due to start early in the morning. Something was bubbling in the office but the information on what was happening was being kept on close hold. I was told the minimum of information but was informed that if anything happened I would be going as nobody else was available. Sounds familiar.

Usually these types of warnings and events fizzle out to nothing and there was no reason to suspect that this would be any different.

I set off for Abbey Wood and arrived early evening and checked into the hotel, went for something to eat and then retired to my hotel room.

I woke up the following morning, had breakfast and moved the car into the Abbey Wood visitors' car park and strolled across the road to the reception area. As I was booking into the site my mobile phone rang and it was the EOD RO asking me to call A5 Plans at HQ Air Command as the bubbling event was now boiling.

I was told that I needed to be at Heathrow airport by 2000 hrs that evening and needed to have a few days' kit, body armour and helmet packed into a civilian bag or suitcase. My kit was at home (three hours away) so I set off immediately to collect it and then made my way to Marham, where I had to visit the medical centre and the admin office to collect the relevant paperwork and a week's supply of malaria tablets. I still did not know where I was going. I picked up my paperwork and someone from the RO then took me to Heathrow airport, where I was to meet up with the rest of the team from Air Command. I arrived in good time but realised that in all of my rushing around I had forgotten to pick up my malaria tablets that had been prescribed for me.

I met up with the recce team leader and the rest of the team and was briefed on what we were going to do. It was still very low key and hush hush so I was told that I could phone home to let my family know that I was going away for up to a week but could not tell them where I was going. I called Dawn and told her to watch the news on TV as that should give her some idea as to where we would be. Business class on British Airways is a great way to travel, especially after the frantic thirty-six hours of driving round the country I had just had but it was necessary as we would be getting straight to work as soon as we landed in Entebbe, Uganda.

Once we had landed we were met by the movements people and taken to our hotel on the shore of Lake Victoria. We had a team briefing and this was our first opportunity to properly meet the other members of the team. We had a team leader from the A5 Plans office at Air Command, a Regiment Officer (my flight commander from IOT), a Hercules pilot, two Royal Engineers, two Tactical Communications personnel, a medic and me. I was relieved that we had a medic with us as she would obviously have some spare malaria tablets in her pack-up to replace the ones I had left in the medical centre at Marham. Not the case unfortunately, she just had a basic first aid kit, so I was going to have to hope I didn't meet any mosquitos during the trip. The communications people set up the comms kit to establish links with the UK and then we all went for a brief from the defence attaché, who had travelled across from Kampala.

At the brief, we were told that sometime in the next couple of days we would be flying by UN helicopter from Entebbe airport to the remote village of Bunia in the north-eastern corner of the Democratic Republic of Congo (DRC). We were to carry out a full recce of the Bunia airfield to ascertain if it was capable of supporting Hercules aircraft that would be supporting a humanitarian mission in the coming months. However, the defence attaché had been informed that there were only five seats available on the helicopter so the first job was to select from the team of nine who would be going into the DRC. Having read the brief and been told of all of the horrors going on in that particular region of the DRC it would have been easy to try and deselect yourself from the recce but as we had travelled all this way to do a job the last thing I wanted to do was sit around hotel for the next few days. The team pretty much selected itself as we needed the Team Leader from A5 Plans, a Hercules Pilot, Force Protection, Royal Engineers to assess the infrastructure and EOD as there was a perceived threat of unexploded ordnance. After a short discussion to finalise the composition of the team it was decided on the five personnel mentioned above and we then went into a more detailed plan of what the following day would bring.

Very early the following morning we jumped on the bus, which took us to Entebbe airport to meet with the UN helicopter crew. We were briefed by the Russian pilot that we would have to sit in the back of the helicopter with our seat belts fastened for the duration of the ninety-minute flight. All very professional and focused, like you would expect from any pre-flight briefing. We drove out to the aircraft parking area and were met by the sight of a very ageing and worn out looking Sikorsky helicopter. We all looked at each other in a mix of amazement, fear, trepidation and above all just seeking a reassuring word from someone.

We climbed on board, strapped ourselves in and waited for take-off. The cargo/passenger compartment of the helicopter was completely empty apart from the five of us, so we started to wonder why our team had been limited to just five. However, when you take into consideration the countries involved in the negotiations to make this recce happen, and the politics of the UN, it was probably just part of the brinksmanship games that often seem to dominate this type of operation. Once we had reached our transit height the pilot came back and asked us if we would like to go into the cockpit. We all said yes, assuming that we would be taking turns to go up front but he ushered us all in, got out some deckchairs and we all sat down and surveyed the tropical landscape below.

As we flew over Lake Albert and crossed the border into the DRC the atmosphere on board the helicopter became more tense and the tension only increased as we started our decent into Bunia airport. We landed and were met by some UN observers who had been in the country for some time and would be our guides for the duration of our visit. As we clambered out of the helicopter the pilot waved us goodbye and shouted, 'I should be back about 1600 hrs'. None of us were happy that the word 'should' had now to crept into his vocabulary and hoped that it was just a figure of speech. The helicopter climbed above us and headed off back towards the border with Uganda.

Our guides gave us a quick briefing on the dos and don'ts of our visit and started by telling us about a local security firm who were guarding the airfield. They had arrived some months ago but had somehow upset the local militia and although they were still guarding the airport, they were also effectively prisoners there as they had been threatened with death if they were caught outside the airfield.

I went out onto the runway with the Royal Engineer as I needed to check for signs of unexploded ordnance and he needed to check for the condition of the runway surface. There was no sign of any UXO or even any damage caused by exploding ordnance. The runway surface was OK in the middle three-quarters but the ends of the surface were badly rutted from heavy aircraft turning on the overheated tarmac. Whilst we had been in one of our briefings a medium-sized transport aircraft had landed but we had not seen who had got out of it. As we were measuring the tarmac depth of the runway we heard somebody shout to us in the broadest Glaswegian accent. We turned around to see a couple of guys in French Foreign Legion uniform, armed to the teeth and asking us to move to one side of the runway. We had a chat to ascertain who was who and who was doing what. They explained that they were just two of many Scots in the Foreign Legion and that they had just got off the transport plane that landed earlier and were carrying out a recce and posting guards around the airfield. These guys and their comrades looked the part and it was obvious that nobody from the warring factions was going to mess with them. I never thought I would ever say this but I was extremely pleased to see the French forces deploying around the airfield to provide security, a far better option than the security firm who had been guarding the area as prisoners.

We then went for a drive around the local area to both orientate ourselves with the environs and also continue to get the up to date information on the current situation in the region. There were villages that were completely uninhabited as the villagers had been driven out or murdered by the tribal wars and there were miles and miles of plastic sheet and tarpaulin campsites that were being supervised by a UN peacekeeping force. I had seen this type of humanitarian refugee disaster whilst in Kosovo but it was nothing on this scale. We were briefed in the UNHQ about the current situation and this gave us the opportunity to ask lots of questions to help inform the recce report that we would be compiling. From the EOD point of view there had been a small amount of booby trapping of homes with grenades and mines and some low-level mortar and RPG attacks but nothing more. As we walked out of the UN HQ we were met by the senior French officer, a full colonel, who seemed rather less than best pleased to see us. I suppose the last thing he expected to see as he arrived at a UN HQ in the DRC was five RAF officers as his welcoming party. But hey, it's not like we were both members of NATO or the UN Security Council, is it?

After leaving the UN HQ we went to visit the base of the UN peacekeepers, who were from a South American country. Why do we have UN peacekeepers from South America you might ask? A very good question but suffice to say that the country's government receives money from the UN for providing forces to carry out this type of task. No matter how effective, or not, they are. On arriving at their base, we saw a huge hangar and on looking inside we saw endless lines of bunk beds littered with personal kit and uniform. It looked as though they had just arrived and were in the middle of establishing their accommodation, but it materialised that they had been here for several months and had made no effort to improve their living conditions. Portable toilets were stacked up outside the hangar but not in use as nobody had bothered to get them up and working, so all ablutions were done in the jungle. It was also rumoured that the peacekeepers were not taking their malaria tablets as catching malaria and returning home was a better option than staying in this hell hole. That reminded me that I still didn't have any malaria tablets!

We had seen all we needed to now and returned to the airport to wait for our transport back to Entebbe. At 1600, as promised, the UN helicopter landed and we climbed aboard and set off back. After landing we were bussed back to the hotel to give an immediate brief to the defence attaché and then to Air Command via the secure comms back to the UK.

The following day we were watching the news and it was reported that there had been street-to-street fighting in Bunia town with rival factions and the French Foreign Legion involved. What a difference twenty-four hours makes. Any operation to support this humanitarian effort could be carried out either from Entebbe or from Bunia itself but there would be no need for any RAF EOD involvement. The operation did happen and was called Operation Artemis. Once the UK had confirmed that they had all the information they needed we were thanked by the defence attaché for our input and we returned to the UK the following day.

Not long after returning to the UK there were rumours that the EOD Role Office would be moving to RAF Wittering, which was great news for almost everyone in the office as most of us lived in the Wittering area and it would cut down on our one-hour each way daily commute. There were also rumours that the USAF were changing the format of the Phoenix Readiness course and that it might cut down on the opportunity for the RAF to take part. The wing commander decided he would travel to the USA to have a meeting with his counterpart to try to secure the future of RAF participation on the course. He would be accompanied by the Role Officer training specialist to look at the training aspects of the course and me as the EOD specialist. The training specialist dropped out of the trip at the last minute due to personal circumstances, leaving me and the wing commander to review the course. This was not too onerous as my time in charge of the Training Flight on 5131 (BD) Squadron meant I was adequately qualified and experienced to do so. The trip involved a weekend in Washington DC before driving up to Fort Dix for the review meetings. This was my first visit to the US capital and gave me enough time to do the military tourist essentials and visit most of the sights.

It was obvious from the early stages of our meetings at Fort Dix that the radical changes being made to the Phoenix Readiness course would make it almost impossible for RAF EOD to attend in the future. There was no time in the new programme to carry out cross training on US equipment and the exercise phase was now going to be assessed towards a unit's preparedness for deploying on operations. It was difficult to imagine that any American commander was going to let some Brits, most of whom would be new to the American equipment and way of operating, take part in an operational assessment of their unit.

We were informed that the exercise would also be changing location from the ranges of Fort Dix to a disused naval air station close by called Lakehurst. We were taken for a drive out to see the new location and as we drove around I noticed a large memorial on the ground. I asked our American hosts what it was and they replied that it was where some airship had crashed some years ago and wasn't anything interesting. After we had finished our tour of the area we had a bit of time to kill so I asked if we could go back and visit the memorial I had spotted earlier in the day. As I approached I read the information plaque and it was only a memorial to the Hindenburg disaster, which occurred on 6 May 1937 and killed thirty-six people. 'Nothing really interesting!'

We made a few inquiries while we were there about any other possible training courses that would allow us to operate with our number one ally and the one that seemed to sound the most promising was something called the Global Anti-Terrorism Operational Readiness (GATOR) course. More to follow later.

Once back at Marham it was clear that the Gulf War was all going to plan and that it was getting close to the time for nominating replacement teams and commanders, although the numbers would be greatly reduced. It was also becoming clearer that the Role Office move to Wittering was becoming a distinct possibility. I was chosen from a cast of one to be the next SO3 EOD in the Divisional HQ, which was now based at Basrah airport. After a few days of pre-deployment training it was time to fly out to the Iraqi city for what was planned to be a four-month tour of duty with every likelihood that I would be leaving from Marham but returning to Wittering.

Chapter 16

Iraq

I arrived at Basrah in the dead of night and was met by my predecessor, who showed me to a transit bed and said he would meet me later for breakfast and we would start the handover. After a couple of hours' sleep we started the process in earnest. The plan was to compress the three-day handover into a few hours as he was hoping to catch the flight back to the UK that evening. As I had previously worked in an Army Brigade HQ in Kosovo the step up to a Divisional HQ wasn't going to be that difficult and we started off with me being introduced to the rest of the Divisional HQ EOD team; the boss, who was an SO2 (major) from the RLC, the Weapons Intelligence WO from the RLC and an electronic countermeasures (ECM) advisor from the Royal Signals.

After the introductions were complete, my predecessor took me down to the armoury, where we signed out our weapons and some ammunition and he told me that we would be going to Basrah Palace to meet the Brigade HQ EOD personnel. He told me that I would be 'top cover' in our Land Rover for the transit to the palace. I asked what that particular task entailed and he explained that my job was to stand up in the back of the open-top vehicle with my weapon loaded and maintain a vigilant watch during our journey. I should raise any security concerns with the commander and driver in the front seats. Not something I was familiar with or had been trained for but 'hey ho, here we go'.

As we drove into Basrah city the roads started to get busier and the traffic slowed down to a walking pace. In true British style, we stopped at all traffic lights and obeyed all traffic signals, which did little for my peace of mind. After less than twelve hours in Iraq, I was stood up in the back of a vehicle, with a loaded gun, surrounded by goats and locals who were all milling through the city but far too close to our vehicle for my liking. After about forty minutes we made it to the palace. I was shown around, met the key personnel and then it was time to return to the Divisional HQ and a reverse run of our trip out. Deep joy.

Once back at the airport we took a drive around the perimeter and went to meet the key units that were based there and then he took me to the permanent living accommodation. I took over my bed space in the large air-conditioned tents and familiarised myself with the toilet and shower units, and in all it was all quite civilised and comfortable. Over a cup of coffee my predecessor made sure that I was happy with the information he had given me and then I took him to the air terminal so he could catch his flight out that evening. Not bad work; a three-day handover completed in less than twelve hours.

The following day I started work in earnest, looking to see what the priority tasks were, and I began organising a routine and a pecking order for these. The first job to tackle was sorting out the task register and, in parallel to sending the high-priority tasks to the EOD teams, to start ticking off those on the register that had never been confirmed or closed down.

There were reports of numerous ammunition caches or storage areas that had never been checked or confirmed. As the EOD teams were very busy with the routine and high-priority EOD tasks, I decided that a few times a week I would get a team together from the Divisional HQ and drive out to check the areas that had been reported, mainly on the initial entry into Iraq. Many of the sites we went to either had nothing there or had been completely destroyed either during the entry phase or by locals searching for anything that could be useful to them.

On numerous sites we turned up to find the area littered with explosive propellant where locals had decided to take the brass casing for its potential value and had discarded the contents. In some areas, we found hidden explosive storage buildings containing all sorts of ordnance from artillery rockets to air-to-air missiles to torpedoes. Much of this ordnance had obviously been used as payment or was received as such by Saddam's regime as there were items that the regime never even had the vehicles to use them from, be it launchers, aircraft, ships or submarines.

We went to one location that had been described as a shipping container full of ammunition but when we got there the ordnance had been scattered as far as the eye could see but all the sides and top of the container had been removed; it was probably taken to repair or build houses or shelters.

Once we had ticked off all the sites that we could drive to easily, we drew up a list of those that were widely dispersed and requested a helicopter flight to try and at least assess them from the air if possible. We had a map and a list of sites, and we set off in a Lynx helicopter with the side doors removed to see what we could find. Most sites could be quickly discounted as we flew over them and this method of recce proved to be invaluable.

However, at one site, a disused heliport south of Basrah, we saw some suspicious buildings and even more suspicious behaviour from some locals, who appeared to be looting the site. The helicopter co-pilot saw somebody with what looked like a man-portable missile launcher running into the cover of one of the buildings. He started screaming at the pilot to take evasive action as he believed the individual was about to fire a missile at us. As the helicopter bucked and weaved from side to side I was getting some great views of first the ground and then the sky out of the open side door of the Lynx. I caught a glimpse of the suspicious individual below and he appeared to be carrying a section of drainpipe. I passed on my observations to the cockpit but they still deemed it to be a missile launcher and carried on with the evasive manoeuvres as we exited the area. By this time, I was feeling extremely sick and was pleased that we were now returning to Basrah airport.

It was during the first couple of weeks in the job that I became even more acutely aware of the mistrust and animosity that existed between the Royal Logistics Corps Ammo Techs and the REs. My boss (the RLC SO2) had been drawing up some policy documents and had sent them to the Permanent Joint Headquarters (PJHQ) for comment and approval. One day when he was away the documents came back with some suggested amendments. I knew that my boss would not agree to the changes, so I called PJHQ to discuss the issues. The RE SO2 in PJHQ agreed to make the changes we discussed and return the document for comment.

As soon as the document was returned I started to read through it to make sure that both I and my boss would be happy with it. The phone rang and it was PJHQ demanding that the document was returned immediately as approval and sign off was imminent. I stated that as soon as I had read through it and was happy with the content I would return it and not before. I was told that it was exactly as we had discussed and that it should be returned for approval within the next thirty minutes. Again, I stated that it would take as long as it took to read and agree the content. As I read through the document it became evident that the changes we had agreed had not been incorporated and PJHQ were simply trying to push through the RE agenda in the absence of my RLC boss hoping to get it signed off as policy before he had the chance to change it. I called PJHQ to question why our changes had not been incorporated and I was told that it was not my place to question PJHQ and that I should return it with full agreement immediately. I pretended that there was interference on the line and that led to us being cut off, which gave me time to continue reading and pick out more changes that had not been agreed. As soon as my boss returned I briefed him on the day's events and the phone conversations that had taken place and he was, quite rightly, incensed. He called PJHQ and the two of them went at it hammer and tongs for ten minutes on the phone with numerous accusations of cap badge rivalry and unprofessionalism. This was one of many similar incidents that I encountered throughout my career but on this occasion I sided with my RLC boss as we were the ones in the operational theatre and the ones who would have to abide by and police the policy that was being produced.

Later that week we were contacted by one of the Dutch EOD teams, who reported that they had found some artillery shells that appeared to be full of liquid and wanted us to get the Defence Chemical, Biological, Radiological and Nuclear (CBRN) Regiment, who were based at Basrah, to go out to their location and carry out some tests. I walked across to the airport fire station where the CBRN Regiment had set up their HQ and was impressed by the set-up they had with comfortable surroundings and a large rubber plunge pool for cooling off during the long hot days. I explained what the Dutch team had reported and that they seemed a bit unsure what to do. They said that they could go out and see if it was leaking; I told them that we could do that and what I wanted was for them to gain entry into the shells and carry out tests to see what they contained. They said that they couldn't do that but if the items were leaking they could seal them up. I said that we could do that as well and that I needed them to do the part of the task that we were not cleared to carry out. They said that they were unable to do anything other than what they had described so I just told them to get back in their pool and we would sort it out ourselves. I was not really sure why they were there other than to try and justify their existence. We advised the Dutch team to bury the items until a safe disposal method and location could be identified. Several weeks later the items were destroyed.

After a few weeks when the pace of life settled down I decided to go to the Divisional HQ bar one evening with my colleagues. The bar was run on a no-profit basis and had the usual two-can rule to ensure there was no unruliness. With lots of senior personnel in the Divisional HQ it was a fairly easy place to regulate as there were enough of us around to ensure that the juniors did not step out of line.

On my last detachment to the USA I had bought myself some 'Air Force' T-shirts and saw this occasion as the perfect time to wear one as the only RAF person in the Divisional HQ. Within seconds of getting into the bar I was approached by some Army bloke, who told me that the bar was only for Divisional HQ personnel and that if I wanted a drink I should go the RAF Bar. I pointed out that I worked in the Divisional HQ but it took a lot of back-up from my work colleagues to convince him that I was telling the truth. What a chopper.

Although we had really started to make an impression on the task list, the number of outstanding ones was still a lot higher than I liked. The EOD Group's OC came into the Divisional HQ one day to ask us if we would like to sponsor some members who would be doing a charity Everest climb the following week. He explained that the teams would be taking it in turns to use stepping machines and other gym equipment to climb the equivalent of the height of Everest. I suggested that instead they should do some charity EOD tasks and see how many they could tick off in a twenty-four-hour period. My suggestion went down like a lead balloon. He didn't see the funny side of my request and never came back again.

The NGOs had started to come into theatre to start clearing areas and buildings as part of the humanitarian mission and had let it be known that they would be carrying out regular meetings. I thought nothing of this until one morning when I got to my desk and my boss said that we would be going to an NGO mine action group meeting later that day.

He told me that we would have to travel in civilian attire as the meeting was being held in a hotel in Basrah city. He then mentioned that we should take our pistols out of the armoury and some ammunition just for security. We were met at the main gate of Basrah airport by a beaten up civilian car – they were all like that – and we climbed in the back and started to make our way into the city. As we drove through the backstreets I was getting a little nervous and asked my boss if this was normal and who knew where we were going? He said he had not told anyone where we were going but not to worry as everything would be OK. My mind now started to work overtime; nobody knew where we were going, we were dressed in civilian clothing with 9mm pistols stuffed in our waistband of our trousers and were being driven through the backstreets of Basrah in a beaten up old car. What could possibly go wrong!

As we drove down a backstreet in the depths of the city we approached some large steel gates that protected the hotel surrounds. The gates were opened by some locals and as we drove inside the compound the gates closed behind us. We entered the hotel and were ushered towards a conference room, where we were served with the very sweet coffee drank by the locals, and we were then shown to a couple of vacant seats around the conference table.

An American chap was chairing the meeting of those de-mining companies that had entered Iraq and me and my boss as the regional military representatives were there to give local knowledge, including the go and no-go areas that were of particular concern to us. The meeting passed off uneventfully with an agreement to carry out future meetings at monthly intervals. We climbed back into the battered old car that had brought us to the hotel and set off back to Basrah Airport, where we were dropped off at the main gate. As we strolled back to the accommodation area to get changed, I turned to my boss and said, 'If you ever put me in a situation like that again, I will kill you.' He looked at me in disbelief as what we had done was not out of the ordinary for his world but it was a million miles away from my comfort zone.

One afternoon we were summoned to a meeting at the Brigade HQ in Basrah Palace, where an Iraqi colonel was looking for some promises of future employment with the British military. He told us he had lots of information regarding weapons and ammunition stores and that if we employed him and his cronies he would help us to find them and destroy them. We stated that we were not in a position to employ him but if he gave us the information we would follow it up and if it turned out to be correct we would see what we could do with respect to getting him some employment with the NGOs. He refused to give us the information and at that point we left the meeting.

A few days later we got a call from the main gate at Basrah airport stating that an Iraqi colonel was at the gate and he had come to see my boss as he said he had promised him some work. I started to explain how this was not the case when my boss interrupted to say that he might have inadvertently offered him something during a phone conversation earlier that day. He asked me to go to the gate to try to defuse the situation and get rid of the colonel once and for all.

As I approached the gate I could see the colonel with half a dozen individuals standing off to one side of the vehicle checkpoint where they had been told to wait. As I approached them the colonel recognised me from our previous meeting and he smiled and shook my hand as if we were long-lost friends. He asked me what work I had for him and his team and how much they would be getting paid. I went on to explain that there was no work and that he had obviously misunderstood the conversation he had had with my boss earlier in the day. He started to get very angry and was shouting and gesticulating furiously and demanded to see my boss immediately. I explained that it was not possible as he was away but he was having none of it and continued with his tirade and the RAF Regiment guards at the checkpoint came forward to ask if there was any trouble that needed sorting out. I shook the colonel's hand and asked him to leave. I then asked the guards not to let him on to the base and to turn him away if he ever turned up again. Problem solved!

Movement around Basrah was navigated by the use of a 'spot map', with every major road being allocated a colour and every major junction given a number. This meant that pre-travel briefings were quick, accurate and easy to understand, with the route being identified by colours and numbers. On one trip into Basrah Palace from the airport we identified the route and set off in convoy as planned. As we drove through the gates of the palace complex, the IEDD vehicle was on its way out to investigate several explosions that had recently taken place in the city. When we got to the Brigade EOD control desk it materialised that four explosions had gone off in the city in the last twenty-five minutes and three of them had been at spot junctions that had been on our route through the city. We could not have missed each one by more than five minutes and was a clear demonstration of how much of a part luck played in your survival in these highly volatile areas of operation.

During the actual bombing campaign, leading up to the entry into Iraq, there were several munitions that did not work as advertised and it became general knowledge that some of them were still lying around Baghdad. A defence contractor in the UK was keen to recover key components from their unexploded munitions and made enquiries about the possibility of putting together a mission to try to recover them.

Phase one of this operation would be to locate them and assess them for recovery, and it was decided that I would get the details and travel to Baghdad to liaise with the US Army EOD personnel. After a roller coaster of a Hercules flight out of Basrah and into Baghdad I was met by a US Army EOD team and taken to the accommodation, where I settled myself down for the evening. The following morning, I went to the HQ, where I was introduced to the teams I would be working with for the next two days and then we all had a briefing on what we were going to do and how we were going to do it. After the briefing, we climbed into our Humvee vehicle (one in a convoy of six), surrounded by cool boxes full of Gatorade and set off for the city.

Convoying with the US military was a totally different experience to doing it with the UK but I must admit it was one that left me feeling much safer. No waiting at traffic lights while locals mill around your vehicle; instead vehicles in the convoy took turns to block routes and intersections as the others leapfrogged through the streets. Not everybody's cup of tea in a hearts and minds campaign but one that got my vote.

We headed first to a rendezvous (RV) point with other EOD teams who had a local knowledge of the areas into which we were going. This was a well-known Baghdad landmark, the Al Shaheed Monument, which was like a split onion. We met the team and set off for the first location, the old MoD HQ, which had two of the failed ordnance items in it. One was embedded in the roof and another was in the basement. The one on the roof was readily accessible but very open to the rest of the city with a major road and hospital close by, and as we made our way to the basement I encountered a very strange scenario. There was a gentleman living in the partially destroyed building, with curtains separating the corridors and rooms, and he welcomed us to his abode and ushered us towards the basement. In the basement was another of the failed munitions. It had obviously hammered its way through several floors before becoming lodged in the ceiling of the basement. After checking these two munitions we went to another building in the centre of the city where a third munition was lying on the roof of the building; again, easy to access.

We then went to another location that had been identified as having a munition on its roof but on climbing to the top of the building there was nothing there. I was unsure as to how old the information was that we were operating from but whatever had been on this building was no longer there. It was likely that it had either been taken by someone for intelligence gathering or to use as an IED or truck bomb.

On the convoy back to the US HQ we were flagged down by some locals who had seen an item of ordnance in the river that ran parallel to the road. We stopped to take a look and saw a large artillery shell lying on the shallow river bed and after setting up a cordon at both ends of the road we pulled the item out, took down the details for the task log and destroyed it. We arrived back at the HQ in time for supper and the following morning I bid goodbye to my hosts and set off on the roller coaster Hercules flight back to Basrah via Al Amarah.

There was a huge effort building right across the country to locate and make safe as many of the ammunition sites as possible that were dotted around the landscape, and to catalogue the serviceable ammunition for handover to the Iraqi Army and destroy the ammunition that was in a state of disrepair. The initiative was being driven by the US HQ in Baghdad as it was estimated that there were thousands of tonnes of ammunition and explosives still lying around the country unguarded. The process was titled Captured Enemy Ammunition (CEA) and was one of the top priorities of the US-led coalition. They were in the process of contracting the task out to a civilian company who were experienced in weapon range and area clearance in the USA. Most of the sites that were being looked at were in the north of the country but there was a proposal to establish one in the south and it quickly became my number one task to liaise with the US HQ, identify a suitable site and assist putting the wheels in motion to establish it as quickly as possible.

I identified a site south of Basrah city and passed the details to Baghdad, and they sent a small team from their HQ to look at it prior to it being approved. They arrived at Basrah and I hosted them for a couple of days, showing them around the local area and visiting the proposed site, which they were extremely happy with. We discussed what it would take to get the site up and running and how many personnel they would need to get it operational in a short space of time. Once they had agreed to the location, a team from the contractors was flown out to start making the more detailed plans of establishing the base as a CEA site, and to make security arrangements and support arrangements with the Divisional HQ at Basrah.

The contract team were very experienced and had been doing this type of work for many years, however they had never done it in a war zone and had never done it in such an austere environment; there would be steep learning curves ahead for everybody. Contracts in place, personnel nominated, it was all systems go to set it up.

It was decided that on the evening before the CEA infrastructure was due to turn up we would clear and protect the base area. To do this we needed support from one of the infantry units, so it was agreed that a small team from the Divisional HQ EOD cell would travel to the base to make sure everything was in order and then the infantry would take over at dusk to provided security overnight and hand over the area to the contractors the following morning.

I set off with a team of six (me, WISWO, ECM advisor and three junior ranks) from the Divisional HQ to check the base area and once we were happy that it was clear we took up post on a vantage point that gave us a view of the whole area and waited for the infantry to turn up.

As it started to get dark nobody had arrived so we made contact with the Divisional HQ and then the Brigade HQ and were told that the infantry unit had decided that they didn't want to sit around all night in the dark so had decided not to bother sending anybody out. Marvellous! After a great deal of discussion about who was best placed to secure an area at night (HQ staff or Infantry) it was agreed, again, that the infantry unit would deploy ASAP. It was now pitch dark and about an hour after the discussion concluded we saw lights approaching from the main road. There was a good chance that this would be the infantry call sign but you could never be too sure, so we took up defensive positions and waited for the vehicles to approach. As they got closer it was obvious that they were military vehicles so we stepped out to welcome them and hand over the mission of securing and protecting the area. We then returned to Basrah airport after what had been another very long, frustrating and stressful day.

The following morning, we returned to the CEA site to meet the contractors and help get them established as best we could. Several 40ft lorries arrived with generators, marquee tents and lighting on board. However, they had not ordered a forklift truck so nothing could be taken off the trailers. Luckily one of the drivers said he knew somebody in the nearest town that had a forklift so the CEA contractors headed off into the town with the driver and some cash to try and hire it for a couple of days. They returned quickly with the forklift following and set about unloading the trailers. The marquees were provided as a package with a group of locals who would erect them, and all seemed to be going well now. Generators and lights were unloaded and placed in the appropriate position but then they realised that they did not have any fuel for the generators, so another trip to the local town was needed to hire a fuel bowser.

Around lunchtime four vehicles arrived and out of them clambered a load of American security contractors, all with shaven heads and beards and dressed in black and wearing sunglasses (I know you shouldn't stereotype but sometimes it's hard). However, there seemed to be one vital ingredient missing in that nobody had a weapon. We spoke to the head of security, who stated that they had not received clearance to bring their weapons into the country and were hoping that we could do something for them.

I pointed out that if they had told us earlier we might have been able to sort something out but it would be difficult now as we only had a few hours of daylight. We drove to Shaibah Logs Base, which had numerous units operating from it, managed to make contact with one of the infantry unit QMs and explained our predicament to him. He had some boxes of brand-new AK-47s and ammunition that had been liberated during the entry into Iraq that he could let us have on a short-term loan. This was the ideal solution to our problem and we signed the items off him and transported them back to the CEA site. We signed them over to the security contractors, who then set about teaching each other how to use the weapon. Scary! Everything now seemed to be going OK on the camp so we left them all to it and headed back to Divisional HQ with a promise that we would return in a couple of days to see how they were getting on.

As we drove towards the site a few days' later it all looked very impressive with the marquees erected and large sand bunds had been constructed to provide security with single entry points that could be guarded easily.

However, as we walked towards the accommodation tent we heard lots of moaning and groaning and looked inside to witness a scene of carnage. There had been a biblical scale breakout of diarrhoea and vomiting and virtually everybody in camp was affected. I spoke to one of the supervisors, who explained that they were all unable to operate and had no idea why the breakout had occurred or how to control it. As I mentioned earlier, these contractors were used to operating in mainland USA and not in austere environments.

The living accommodation was adjacent to the messing/admin accommodation and in between the two they had put the toilets and the rubbish bins. They were eating in the living accommodation and leaving waste food lying around under beds, with no hand cleansing gels or wash facilities for use when entering the relevant areas. It was a recipe for disaster that had very quickly developed into a nightmare scenario. We gave them a few tips on how to rearrange the camp set-up, with toilets and bins being placed on the remote extremities of the area and establishing clean areas and routines, and then left them to it.

Back at Div HQ we received a call the following day from the CEA site explaining that two of the staff were extremely ill and that they needed to be evacuated to a medical facility. I spoke to the Divisional HQ watch-keeper about the possibility of getting one of the Medical Emergency Response Team (MERT) helicopters to fly to the site and evacuate them to the hospital at Shaibah. He said that there weren't any available (there were), it was not his responsibility to evacuate civilian contractors and therefore he would not task the MERT helicopter. I tried to reason with him, stating that the safety and well-being of the CEA teams was paramount to the success of the CEA programme and was a very high priority for the US-led coalition. He still refused to task the team.

I emailed the head of the CEA programme in Baghdad, explaining the lack of support being provided by the Divisional watch-keeper and expressing my concerns over the safety of the CEA personnel.

For information, I also copied the email to the watch-keeper, who immediately came over to my desk and started screaming and shouting and telling me how unprofessional I was to write this email – and then agreed to task the helicopter. I pointed out that not tasking the helicopter in the first place was the unprofessional act, not writing an email.

The following day we went back to the site to check on the welfare of the contractors and as we arrived several of the security contractors were in the process of handing back their guns and ammunition as they had had enough of living in squalor and had decided to leave. They were planning to get dropped off at the border with Kuwait and make their own way back to the USA.

Baghdad recce carried out, CEA site up and running, the pace of life was starting to slow down in the Divisional HQ and there was a huge push to quickly convert what had been a UK Military HQ into a Multi-National Divisional HQ for the South East of Iraq (MNDSE). As with all multinational HQs, there needed to be a good spread of nationalities across all of the disciplines and it was decided that there needed to be a multinational flavour to the EOD cell. It couldn't be the boss or the weapons intelligence WO or the ECM advisor, so that left the SO3 post.

I must admit I wasn't overly disappointed to be short toured and felt that I had achieved a great deal in my three months in the Divisional HQ and when my Estonian replacement arrived I handed over the reins in a couple of days and made my way to the air terminal for my flight home.

Chapter 17

Explosive Ordnance Disposal (EOD) Role Office Wittering

On returning to the UK the Role Office had moved back to RAF Wittering, so the one-hour commute to work had now been reduced to fifteen minutes and my new office was in the old 5131 (BD) Squadron building that I had occupied during my time standing in as OC Operations Flight on 5131 (BD) Squadron.

My first job was to carry on where I left off, looking for some training opportunities with the USAF, and I made some enquiries with some of my contacts in the USA about the GATOR course. The Global Anti-Terrorism Operational Readiness (GATOR) course was run at Redstone Arsenal in Huntsville, Alabama, and was a prerequisite for all US EOD operators to undertake prior to going on operations in either Iraq or Afghanistan.

It sounded like it was worth a shot, so we made contact with the US Embassy and arranged to travel out to Huntsville to have a look at the course. We arrived in Huntsville and were met by the US Embassy representative, who drove us to Redstone Arsenal. As we approached the security gate we slowed down and the embassy representative explained to the security guards that we were RAF officers and were on a short visit sponsored by the US Department of Defense (DoD). The security guard was in autopilot and said, 'Sir, I need the foreign nationals to get out of the car.' The embassy representative was mortified and explained to the security guard that we were not foreign nationals but were from the UK military, the USA's closest ally. The security guard said, 'Sir, I need the foreign nationals to get out of the car.'

It was obvious at this point that there was no flexibility so we got out of the car with the embassy representative apologising every thirty seconds for the way we were being treated, but we calmed him down and explained that we understood and that the security guards were only doing their job as briefed.

A couple of days later we realised that we had taken a wrong turn on our journey between meeting locations and were heading out of one of the security checkpoints and had no option but to drive out and do a U-turn to re-enter.

As we passed the checkpoint on the way out we stopped and spoke to the security guards and explained what we had done and that we were going to do a U-turn and come back through the security point. 'No problem sir he replied.' We did a U-turn about 50 yards from the gate and drove back towards the checkpoint. As we pulled up the guard looked at our ID cards and said, 'Sir as you are foreign nationals I need you to get out of the car'. We tried to reason with him and explained that we had just spoken to him on the way out but he was having none of it and we decided that it was easier just to do as he said.

We had an excellent few days watching the US operators being put through their paces as they prepared for lengthy and arduous tours of the Middle East. However, it quickly became apparent that this was an operational course that used American equipment and American procedures and therefore would not be suitable for UK EOD operators.

One of the greatest innovations we saw on the course was the use of very cheap and readily available radio-controlled cars to destroy roadside bombs. The cars were given the title of BOMBOT and the EOD operators would simply strap an explosive charge to the car, drive it to the suspect package and detonate it. The suspect package would disappear in a cloud of flame and smoke (as would the BOMBOT) but it cleared the area and did not necessitate putting the EOD operator's life in danger. In operational theatres the concept was used extensively until the BOMBOT became susceptible to electronic countermeasures and, like all good ideas, it had to evolve to keep one step ahead of the insurgents.

Soon after the trip to Huntsville I went back to the Falkland Islands for a few days to carry out a review of the EOD capability and shortly after returning from there I was tasked by Air Command to go to the Middle East to carry out an armament investigation into an incident that had happened at Ali Al Salem in Kuwait.

I reported to Air Command for a briefing on the circumstances of the incident and then set off to Brize Norton to catch the flight to Doha in

Qatar, which was the RAF HQ for all Middle East operations. On arrival, I was given another briefing by the senior engineer at Doha and was then taken to my accommodation for a night's rest before flying to Kuwait the following morning. I arrived at Kuwait airport and was met by an MT driver with the transport to take me to Ali Al Salem. As soon as I arrived at Ali Al Salem I was shown to my accommodation and after a quick change into uniform I was taken to the Eng Wg HQ, where I was given an office to use for the duration of my investigation.

Some RAF personnel had been preparing explosives for destruction with some US colleagues who were also based in Kuwait. As they made the explosive ordnance safe for destruction, one of the personnel tried to pull an item from the pile of ordnance; they heard a loud bang and a bullet was discharged, just missing the head of an RAF person and shooting a member of the USAF through the foot. It turned out that the UK version of the particular weapon system involved had 9mm spotting rounds incorporated into system but the US version did not. None of the RAF personnel involved in the task were familiar with the weapons system and none were EOD qualified. Although they had asked Air Command for information and permission they had not asked the EOD Role Office for assistance and therefore no in-depth analysis was done on the type of weapons to be disposed of. By the time I arrived to carry out the investigation, the USAF chap was already walking again, although with a plaster cast on his foot. He had been extremely lucky as the bullet had passed between his toes in the fleshy part of his foot and therefore no bones had been shattered. The RAF person had minor hearing issues due to the proximity of the discharge to their head but it could have been a whole lot worse for both of them. The investigation was wrapped up fairly quickly with a recommendation that the EOD RO should be consulted for all EOD issues; not exactly radical as this is what should have happened in the first place but maybe putting the EOD RO at Air Command with the other Armament RO would help. More on that idea later. I flew back to Doha to debrief the HQ and caught the next available flight back to the UK.

I returned to Wittering having had a frantic few months to find one of the guys in the office had been looking on the internet and identified a UXO forum that was taking place in Bangkok in a few weeks' time.

Nothing ventured, nothing gained. I asked the wing commander if we could attend but he said that whilst he could possibly justify the EOD RO attending the forum, he could only do so for one person. He went on to say that seeing as how I had been rushing all over the globe for the past few months he was happy to let me go as a bit of a reward for my efforts. I felt a little bit guilty as somebody else had found the event but, not one to look a gift horse in the mouth, I set about making arrangements for the trip. It soon came around and I flew to Bangkok to attend the forum, which was very interesting and a complete eye-opener as to how other nations tackled the rising problem of clearing UXO and improvised explosive devices. Whilst I had worked regularly with European and US EOD units, this gave me the opportunity to look at how some of the Asian countries carried out their EOD work.

The conference was being held in the Dusit Thani Hotel in Bangkok and most of the delegates were also staying there, which made it ideal for continuing the days' conversations on into the evening.

The most memorable brief I received was from a Far East delegation, who brought a video that they had taken during a live IED task. It showed two EOD personnel entering a room where a suspicious box had been reported to have been left on a table. As they entered the room the box was clearly visible in the centre of the room and they approached it with caution, only to be followed in by another six people from various different security agencies and the media. As they all looked on, one of the EOD operators started to open the box and it exploded with a huge bang. Several of the people, including the EOD operator, were injured in the blast and although some were seriously hurt, there were no fatalities or critical injuries. I'm not sure what amazed me the most; the fact that they carried out this operation in a room full of people or the fact that they told everybody at the conference what they did.

Not long after returning from Bangkok we arranged to take our group captain to the US EOD intelligence centre at Indian Head in Maryland, USA. We flew to Washington for a couple of days, did some military tourism and then drove to Indian Head to meet our hosts. They had an amazing set-up that was purpose-built for both exploiting ordnance and also for providing a live reach back facility for EOD operators in Iraq and Afghanistan. The reach back facility allowed EOD operators to have a live audio and video feed to the facility at Indian Head over which they could identify ordnance and have access to additional expertise to devise or identify ways to deal with it. Bearing in mind that as a UK EOD capability we often talked of enhancements and improvements in capability costing thousands of pounds; we were having dinner one evening with our host from Indian Head when he received a phone call from the US DoD confirming that he had been successful in securing a multi-million-dollar funding bid for improvements to the reach back facility enabling it to operate 24/7. Visit over, we set off back to the UK having forged even closer ties with a key ally.

Once back in the office it became clear that the OC EOD Engineering Development Investigation Team (EDIT) post was coming available and as the EDIT was part of our overall structure I saw an opportunity to get what was seen as a plum role in the EOD world, and additionally the only operational junior officer post in RAF EOD that I had not done. I asked my boss about the possibility of moving from the Policy job into the EDIT role and she agreed.

The RAF had developed a new exercise concept to replace the individual TACEVALS that units had been subjected to for many years. A complete force package was put together from all different units and they all then deployed in stages to RAF St Mawgan in Cornwall, where they would go through settling in and work up phases before moving on to an assessed exercise. The concept worked really well and I was fortunate enough to have been one of the lead EOD instructors and evaluators for all the exercises that took place.

On one occasion a colleague and I drove the six or so hours to St Mawgan and arrived at the officers' mess to book into our accommodation. As we entered the mess we were approached by the exercise director, who had a face like thunder and was shouting and bawling about how useless the EOD teams were and how they had turned the deployment into a complete shambles. Over a cup of coffee, we tried to calm him down and asked him to tell us what the problems were, promising that we would sort them out. We expected tales of bad behaviour or drunken exploits but he went on to tell us that one of the teams had turned up in a vehicle that had a different number plate to the one that should have been deployed. We listened attentively and apologised for the extreme stress that this had obviously caused him and reaffirmed our commitment to getting to the bottom of the heinous crime that had been committed! The team could have not come at all as their vehicle had broken down before it even left RAF Wittering but they used their initiative and rather than leave a capability gap or turn up late they acquired a replacement. It appears that sometimes you can't do anything right. We gave the situation a stiff ignoring and after a day or so all was forgotten.

Coming up soon was the EOD ABCANZ meeting, which was an annual get together that took place between the EOD communities from America, Britain, Canada, Australia and New Zealand. Previously I had only ever managed to go to the UK-based meetings but this year it was in Auckland, New Zealand, and I put together a case for attending as the new OC EOD EDIT. My case was approved and I was once again over the moon at the prospect of going to New Zealand and taking part.

In parallel, the EDIT was scheduled to provide EOD cover for a weapons trials programme taking place at China Lake in the USA and we were planning to split the EDIT into two, two-men teams to do three weeks each to cover this six-week trial. I worked out that if I covered the second three-week period I could fly to New Zealand for the ABCANZ meeting and then fly back to Los Angeles and drive to China Lake in time for the last three weeks of the trial.

This would necessitate flying to New Zealand by the western route and not the usual eastern route, and whilst the journey out was fairly uneventful it did mean catching interconnecting flights at Los Angeles, which meant having to be locked in a room for two hours with only sparse amenities; similar to Ascension Island but indoors and without the cockroaches.

We arrived in Auckland on schedule and even with five days of conference to attend we still managed to get in our dose of military tourism and saw many of the sights in and around Auckland. ABCANZ over, we set off back to the UK with me scheduled to get off at Los Angeles. My EDIT team partner was due to fly out from the UK and was supposed to arrive in Los Angeles at roughly the same time as me, with the team who were already in China Lake driving down to pick us up. What could possibly go wrong?

Well nothing as it turned out, we all arrived at Los Angeles airport within thirty minutes of each other, which wasn't bad going considering where we had travelled from. We met up at a car hire place and set off on the four-hour journey to the sprawling metropolis that is Ridgecrest and our accommodation. Once settled in we had a couple of days to acclimatise and do all of the admin for the trials such as checking equipment, getting base passes, etc. The two guys we were taking over from gave us a thorough handover and it turned out that their three-week stint had been fairly quiet due to aircraft unserviceability and bad weather. Fortunately for us, that meant that our three weeks should be very busy as everybody tried to play catch up and get the trials completed. This turned out to be the case but, of course, we still had time to do a bit of military tourism visiting Mount Whitney, Trona Pinnacles and Death Valley.

There were two specific weapon phases to the trials that we were supporting. These were Storm Shadow, of which there were two firings planned, and Brimstone, of which there were thirty-five firings planned. The Brimstone trials were first on the programme and the first few firings went without a hitch. The second phase had a few issues in that one of the missiles failed its aircraft check and had to be returned to the testing facility for more in-depth tests to be carried out. The missile failed the test and it had to be destroyed on the range, making this EDIT team the first to destroy an operational Brimstone.

The following day another missile failed the aircraft test and once again had to be taken to the testing facility for further checks. As we carried out this test with the contractor it became obvious it was going the same way as the previous one and we stopped just before the point of no return. We explained to the contractor that it was unusual for two missiles to fail the same test at the same point in the process and that it might be worth trying a new test set or a new test cable. We explained that if we progressed on to the next stage of the test and it failed we would have no option but to destroy the missile as we had done the day before. The contractor was adamant that there was nothing wrong with the test set or the cables and that we should press on; we did and it failed again.

He then said that he would come back the following day with a new test set and test cable and we would run the test again but we pointed out that the servicing schedule stated that if it failed this specific test the missile could not be moved and must be destroyed where it lay. We had advised him and warned him of the consequences, and we then became the first EOD team to destroy two operational Brimstone missiles.

A few days later the trial would be moving to another level and Brimstone missiles would be used against moving armoured vehicles. In the operations room briefing that morning the contractors explained that the target vehicles would be towed across the lake bed targets by remote-controlled armoured vehicles and that the aircraft would launch the missiles at the target that was being towed. Me and my teammate looked at each other in amazement and questioned the trials director on how the missile was going to differentiate between the armoured vehicle target and the armoured vehicle that was towing the target? He flippantly brushed aside our concerns and implied that we were just EOD operators and his trials team had every base covered. At that we found ourselves a grandstand seat in the back of the range operations room and sat back ready to observe the proceedings. The aircraft called in to say that it was approaching the range area and the remote-controlled tank set off across the range towing the target tank. The aircraft reported that it had identified the target and was ready to launch the missile; clearance was given and the pilot declared that the missile had been fired.

An explosion was seen around the turret area of the remote-control tank but it continued to tow the target tank across the range. The explosion had disabled the remote-control gear and now the tank was out of control towing the target tank across the range.

Everybody looked in amazement and shock as we sat and sniggered in the back of the ops room. 'What you need is a tank-stopping missile,' we shouted, our humour went down like a lead balloon as they frantically tried to come up with a plan of how to stop the out-of-control tank convoy. Fortunately for all concerned there were other derelict armoured vehicles scattered around the range area and as the convoy crashed into one of these derelict targets it ground to a halt.

The rest of the Brimstone trials went off without a hitch and we moved onto phase two, the Storm Shadow firings.

Firing number one went satisfactorily from a contractor point of view but from a more critical viewpoint it missed the target by 50m and therefore could hardly be deemed a success in this modern era of smart precision weapons. Before the firing, the range operations people had filled a trench with burning oil and tyres to try and shield the target from the missile and it obviously succeeded to a degree. The contractor stated that the shielding was clearly the reason for the slight miss of the target, to which we responded that it was obviously very accurate unless you were going to drop it in a war zone where buildings would be burning ferociously, and we would never be doing that would we?

The second Storm Shadow firing was far less of a success because as soon as the missile left the aircraft it plummeted straight to the ground, crashing in a remote part of the range. Test firings complete, it was now time to recover the missile that had failed, or at least what was left of it. The following morning all interested parties met at 0600 to travel out to the area of the range that the missile had crashed into to try and recover as much as possible. We got there after about an hour of cross-country driving and spent the next six hours walking up and down the hillside searching for debris. It was very arduous work in the baking Californian sunshine but we managed to recover all the parts that we deemed to be of interest to the contractor and to us as the EOD team.

On arriving back at range ops, we deemed our support to this trial to be over and decided to make arrangements to travel to Nellis AFB, just outside Las Vegas, the following day to do a liaison visit with the USAF EOD teams there to try to arrange some joint training for the future. Just as we were packing away all the debris we had brought back from the hillside crash site, a couple of scientists wandered in from their lazy day and said that there were a couple of pieces from the missile that they needed that we hadn't brought back. We explained that we had brought back everything that we deemed to be either useful or dangerous and that there was very little left on the mountain that could be identified. They were still adamant that there were bits they needed and that we should postpone our trip to Nellis to go and search for them. When we asked why they either A, hadn't told us about the items they needed before we went that day, or B, come out with us at 6 in the morning to find them, they said they had been out drinking the night before and forgot to set their alarm. After that confession, we gave them the contact number of the US range guys who had been with us that day and the GPS co-ordinates of the wreckage, wished them luck with their search and set off for Vegas. Once in Vegas we checked into the hotel and the following morning set off for Nellis AFB to meet with the USAF EOD teams and arranged some joint training for the following year as there were no more range clearance events planned until then.

Whilst on the subject of scientists, the EOD EDIT also attended a trial at Pendine in Wales where the scientists were looking into the effects of missiles that detonated in storage and what affect they would have on missiles stored close by. Our job on the trial was to provide the equipment to detonate the missiles and to make safe anything that was left in a hazardous condition after each trial event.

When we turned up the scientists showed us their pride and joy that they had had manufactured for the trial. It was a large cradle that could be bolted into the ground and onto which the missile could be harnessed. It was a very robust and solid cradle that had obviously taken quite a bit of time and money to manufacture. After looking at the cradle with the missile bolted on to it we asked if they had other cradles to use when this one got destroyed when the missile detonated. They said that they had only had one made as they were convinced it would be strong enough to withstand the blast and fragmentation from the missile detonating. We had a slightly differing view in that we thought that the cradle would be seriously damaged by the first detonation; but there was only one way to find out. We placed another missile close to the harnessed one in order to determine what, if any, impact the detonation would have on a missile stored close by. We retired to the safety of a concrete bunker and watched the events on a CCTV system. On initiation, the missile detonated violently but we were pleased to see that, although the adjacent missile had been subjected to some collateral damage, it had not itself detonated. After a safe waiting time, we went forward to inspect the damage and to set up the scenario again for the next trial. As we predicted, the missile cradle was bent and buckled in all sorts of different ways, so much so that we could not even release the bolts to separate the cradle. There would not be another trial that day as it was going to take hours to release and reconstruct the equipment. We came back the following day to find a couple of less well-engineered cradles that would be sacrificial in the trials.

Back at Wittering, one of the chief techs in the office got notice that he had been selected for promotion but that it would mean moving away from home and traveling back at weekends. He decided that he did not want that style of life and made up his mind to leave the RAF at an upcoming predetermined exit point. We identified a vacant slot on 5131 (BD) Squadron at Wittering that he would be ideally suited for and it would mean that he could continue living at home with his family.

I approached the manning people and explained the situation to them but all I got in return was a blunt response and a request for me to keep my nose out of their business. Their bottom line was that if he wanted promotion he would have to move.

I explained that it was not that simple as he already had preparations for life outside of the RAF and if they did not give him the job at Wittering he would leave and they would have two jobs to fill.

Still no realisation of the impending problems and no understanding that filling one vacant job was better than creating another one.

They were unmoved by our plea, refused to compromise and assumed that these were idle threats that would not come to fruition. In reality it was not a threat but a fact of life; the chief tech left the RAF and manning were in another self-generated pickle!

During my time in the EOD Role Office I was tasked with organising the annual EOD dinner. This function was always held at RAF Wittering as the home of RAF bomb disposal and was normally held in the officers' mess. It was an excellent opportunity for all EOD officers and SNCOs past and present to get together, catch up on the squadron's activities and socialise till the early hours of the morning. The format very rarely changed and the organisation of the dinner flip-flopped between the Role Office and 5131 (BD) Squadron depending on who was in charge of each of those organisations and where they saw their role. The organisation of the event was fairly simple, but very time-consuming. However, it always gave a great sense of achievement when the dinner went well, which of course it always did.

I was told to organise it by my boss and I did. Later, as the boss of 5131 (BD) Squadron we took on the role. I told one of the flight commanders on the squadron to organise it and they did. More recently however, that concept appears to have been lost, with both officers and SNCOs shirking their responsibility and the dinner did not take place in 2017.

I was really enjoying the EDIT job and we were starting to get some invitations to lots of trials and some interesting new weapon projects, with our involvement becoming key to all such events. Then came the phone call that changed everything as I was told that I had been picked up for promotion to squadron leader and was posted to be the RAF desk officer in the newly established Joint EOD & Search Staff Branch (JEODS). Whilst I was sad to be leaving the EOD EDIT, I was over the moon with promotion and couldn't wait to get started in the new job. JEODS was an MoD Department, part of the Directorate of Joint Capability (D Jt Cap), that in true joint service style was located alongside HQ Land Command at Wilton as there was supposedly no room in the MoD main building in London.

This meant that I would have to do weekly commuting to Wilton, near Salisbury, as the family were settled in our own house near Peterborough.

The manning desk officer had one last joker to play and told me that before going to JEODS I would be attending the Senior Logistics Managers Course (SLMC) at RAF Cranwell. The SLMC was a logistics course so I am not really sure why engineers were on it but there were more RAF engineers than logisticians on this particular course. There were also a lot of foreign students and as it panned out the RAF officers were only attending to give it some credibility with them and to do most of the work for projects and planning the station and industry visits.

I arrived at Cranwell having been told that I should stay in the officers' mess as it made for better course cohesion, only to be told after I had moved into the mess that as my family home was less than 50 miles away (it was 38) I would have to pay to live in. I tried to negotiate based on the fact that the course supervisor would prefer me to live in but failed miserably, so I commuted daily from home.

The course consisted of lots of senior officers (mainly loggies) giving briefings, lots of sitting round in armchairs and drinking coffee, lots of station visits, lots of industry visits and a final course project; in all a fairly interesting three months but not of much value.

Our course project was to assess the value of the SLMC course and recommend any changes that could be made to improve it. Suffice to say that the course was decreased in length and modularised soon after.

SLMC ticked off, it was time to pack my car and move to my new home in the officers' mess at Wilton.

Chapter 18

Joint Explosive Ordnance Disposal (EOD) & Search Staff MoD

I arrived at Wilton mid-morning after a tortuous drive through the rush hour traffic on the M40 and around Oxford and moved into my room in the main mess building. I then walked across to the office, where I was met by my wing commander, who had previously been my boss on 5131 (BD) Squadron. He had also been promoted and posted to JEODS as the Chief of Staff (COS) and at this point of the formation of JEODS it was very small and consisted of a Royal Engineer colonel as the head of department, an RAF wing commander as the COS with desk officers from the RN, the RE, the RLC and the RAF. The desk responsibilities were divided, not into single service responsibilities, although that was an implied task, but lines of development. My job at the outset involved responsibility for all EOD and search training and personnel issues across all three services. This had the potential to be an extremely wide-ranging, diverse and interesting job and there would definitely be opportunities to continue on the 'Lunn Policy' travelling around the globe from my time in the RAF EOD RO. It also gave me a much closer insight into the Army cap badge rivalry that I was aware of between the RE and the RLC but had no idea how fierce and bitter it was until this job came along.

Job number one was to try to develop a single training syllabus for the officers' and SNCOs' EOD course that was carried out at the Defence EOD School (DEODS). The RN, RE and RAF were already doing the same course in the same location, so pulling the RLC into this process shouldn't have been too difficult. Or so I thought! They were doing their own course at Kineton and it didn't include everything on the DEODS course, but they were out on the streets doing the same job. It seemed crazy that this was being allowed to happen but every time I thought we were close to achieving the Holy Grail, the RLC would come up with another reason for them not to attend the DEODS course.

The single course idea was parked for a while as the RAF had put forward a proposal to get specialist pay for its EOD operators based on the need to recruit and retain personnel to man all the required RAF EOD posts. We had a close relationship with the RAF EOD Role Office and suggested that the proposal would have more chance of getting approved if it was a joint proposal from all four cap badges involved. It was decided that as the MoD desk officer for EOD personnel issues, I would be the person to pull the joint proposal together and get it approved by the MoD pay review body. The first stage in this process was to get the agreement of the four cap badges as without that we had no chance of it succeeding. The RN agreed to support it even though they would not get EOD pay as they were in receipt of diving pay, the RE agreed to support it as long as they didn't have to do much work towards it and the RAF were in agreement as we had taken their proposal as a starting point. The RLC however were more difficult to convince as they thought they deserved more than anybody else and at one stage declared that they would prefer that everybody got nothing rather than them getting the same as the other cap badges.

It then came to light that they were pressing ahead with their own bid for EOD pay and the senior ranks of all three services had to quickly get together to ensure that that bid was not allowed to make it to the MoD as it was doomed to fail and would take everything else down with it. Their draft proposal had an annual cost of £22.5 million just for the RLC. To put that in context, the proposal that was finally approved in 2008 cost just £2.4 million for RE, RLC and RAF. The £2.4 million was a realistic price to pay for all officer and SNCO EOD operators, especially in a time of operator shortage, but a proposal of £22.5 million would never have made it past the first reading by the pay review body.

In parallel to writing the case to have specialist EOD pay I also took the opportunity to attend several courses to further enhance and widen my knowledge of the full spectrum of EOD and search disciplines. First of all, I attended the NATO EOD staff officers' course, which was delivered by the UK on behalf of NATO. It was a very good basic-level course that taught people how to be staff officers in HQs for multinational operations and gave a good insight into the capabilities of each of the nations that were attending the course. After that I attended a couple of search courses at the National Search Centre (NSC). They were the unit search co-ordinators (USC) course and the unit search advisors (USA) course, and both were very informative. These courses were primarily for Royal Engineers and for me it was a matter of pride to show that the RAF could adapt to and understand the theory and practice of military search techniques. I joked with the instructors and the other course students that search was just about finding things and I had been doing that since I was a small child, so how hard could it possibly be? Much to the dismay of the commanding officer of the NSC (who I knew from previous jobs), I came top of the class.

My role in JEODS gradually developed and gave me the opportunity, as I had hoped, to continue from where I let off in the RAF EOD RO with more travel trips to various destinations.

I was invited to an EOD and detection seminar in Madrid and saw this as another opportunity to get some detailed information on how the scientific world was proposing to tackle the increasing terrorist threat. In parallel to organising my visit to the conference, I checked the football fixtures and saw that Real Madrid were playing at home on one of the nights that I would be there.

This was another excellent chance to see one of the greatest ever football teams playing at home in the Santiago Bernabeu Stadium and was too good an opportunity to miss. This was the Real Madrid team known as the Galacticos, with Carlos, Zidane, Figo, Ronaldo and Beckham playing for them, and it was a great experience to see such a famous chapter in the history of the club.

The conference itself was another great insight into how the scientific mind worked and how it was so often divorced from reality. We had an afternoon study session, during which the scientists from several different countries explained how they were proposing to tackle the problem of identifying suicide bombers by x-raying them as they approached any security checkpoints.

They were extremely passionate and devoted to their ideas, and did not take difficult questions lightly. As they reached the culmination of their briefing they explained how the x-ray machine they were designing would scan all approaching people and immediately sound a warning if any type of explosives were detected. Somebody asked at what distance the machine would work at and they explained that it was 100 per cent accurate at distances up to a metre. The next question tried to tease out what would happen once the alarm sounded as if it was a suicide bomber and he had already got to within a metre of the checkpoint all he had to do was detonate his device and he would have achieved his aim. Once again came a stony silence as the scientists realised that it was a case of back to the drawing board.

Following on from the Madrid seminar I got an invite to a UXO and countermine forum, which was taking place at a hotel and conference centre in Orlando. The conference sounded as if it would have a lot of useful briefings and demonstrations, so I got approval from the boss and made plans to attend. As part of the registration process it turned out that the conference would be preceded by a golf tournament, which would be held on the conference centre's own course. I registered to play and made sure that taking my clubs out with me was not going to present any difficulties. On arrival, the conference delegates were split into teams with single delegates like myself being assigned to teams that had fewer than four players. I was teamed up with some US Army guys and we had a great morning's golf, finishing just in time to get changed and have lunch before the briefings commenced.

There were three very busy days of briefings, presentations and demonstrations with a lot of the information being very useful for developing UK training procedures and area clearance procedures.

One of the briefings was being given by the CEA contractors who I had helped establish in southern Iraq and it was really good to see how their programme had developed from what it was when I left to an operation that was regularly carrying out 100-ton blows of unserviceable ammunition. A couple of the contract supervisors were there and it was a good feeling that they recognised me and we spent a few hours in the evening catching up on life in general. They also offered me a job overseeing some of their overseas projects but I was enjoying my new role and didn't fancy spending more time in the hell holes of the world so I politely declined.

Back at Wilton, I was playing more golf and along with my boss we entered the HQ Land doubles match play event just as a way of us getting out to play more. We won our first few matches fairly easily but then the games, on paper at least, started to look more difficult. However, we were both at the top of our game and carried on with some convincing victories as we made it through several more rounds. Then it started to get serious as we made it through into the final, where we were to play the tournament favourites. We were both still playing really well and saw off our opponents with relative ease. As we revelled in our victory we cleared our diaries to make sure that we would be available for the HQ Land Golf Society annual dinner and presentation evening. There was no way on earth that we were not going to be there as the RAF team to pick up the HQ Land doubles trophy. Some said that our securing the award of EOD pay was our greatest moment in JEODS, but in reality, it came a close second to winning the HQ Land golf trophy.

The GATOR course at Huntsville had been further developed and they had introduced an international version for all NATO countries. Although it still used American equipment, it did not rely on using American procedures, or if it did it used procedures that were easy for other countries to adapt. I was asked to go and validate the course on behalf of the Joint EOD community and in doing so I was told I would be accompanied by an RLC staff officer from the HQ of the Defence Explosives, Munitions and Search School (DEMSS). He spent the whole of the time in Huntsville telling everybody how it was not like that in Northern Ireland and how what they were doing was wrong.

Needless to say, this didn't go down too well with the American instructors on the course or the multinational students, and they tended to just get on with the task in hand and ignore his moaning. The course could have been useful to certain elements of the UK military and although we decided not to send students we did adopt some of the techniques and procedures during our time in Afghanistan.

Not wishing to look another tourist gift horse in the mouth, Huntsville was only four hours' drive away from Memphis, so on my weekend off I drove there to visit Graceland, the home of Elvis Presley.

Shortly after returning from Huntsville, the boss of the Australian EOD School came to visit several of the UK EOD locations to see how we had developed our capability and how we could help one another. The individual concerned had been through the RAF AEOD School at North Luffenham many years earlier when I was OC Training Flight and I arranged to meet him at one of the UK dispersed locations.

When we met he proceeded to tell me how his meeting at HQ DEMSS had been all about how good the RLC were and trying to find out what it was they could do to help improve what the Australians were doing. How condescending. I took a different tack and asked how the Australian EOD structure and capability was developing and how they were succeeding in bringing together their training. 'Why don't you come over and see,' he replied! Another travel opportunity was beckoning and after approaching the subject with the head of JEODS he agreed that I could go under one condition: that he could come, too. After a couple of months exchanging emails and putting together a detailed plan we had a visit arranged that would enable us to visit most of the Australian EOD training establishments and attend a counter-improvised explosive device (C-IED) seminar at the Australian MoD.

We flew to Sydney via Singapore and arrived late in the evening, picked up the hire car and drove into the city to try and find our accommodation for the first few nights. After driving around for some time, we eventually found HMAS Kutabul, which was just a short walk along the coast from the Sydney Opera House and a prime location from which to do some sightseeing.

After a couple of days we drove out to the Australian EOD school at Orchard Hills, where the RAAF did their EOD training, and from there went to the engineers training establishment. After that we drove back to Sydney to HMAS Penguin, where we spent a couple of days with the Australian Navy looking at their training facilities and processes. Once all these training locations had been visited we set off on the long drive to Canberra to attend the C-IED seminar. We were very privileged to have been invited as very few foreign nationals get to attend such events, or so we thought.

As the head of JEODS, my boss was supposed to approve all UK visits to overseas EOD and search events in other countries as a way of cutting down on excessive travelling and also to ensure that any UK delegate was singing from the same hymn sheet as the MoD. You can imagine the surprise on his face as we checked in at the seminar registration desk to see not one, not two, but three senior RLC officers registering for the event. It was difficult to see who was the most surprised at this awkward moment but it was undoubted as to who was in the right and who was not. This incident resulted in greater scrutiny being placed on any future attendance at overseas events and an assurance that all such visits would be approved by the MoD Staff Branch (JEODS). After the seminar was finished we did the obligatory tourism around Canberra and set off back towards Sydney to catch our flight home.

On arriving back in the office, the pace was gathering again on the concept of all four cap badges doing the same course, at the same time, in the same classroom and it was being talked about at the highest levels. Everyone agreed that it was the way ahead; everyone that was except for the RLC, who still thought they were far superior to everyone else. They were adamant they already knew some of the elements taught on the course and therefore didn't see why they should attend them. The course was, and always had been, essentially split into three phases covering maritime, land and air weapons, and the RLC were adamant that they did not need to do the land phase. The Navy attended the maritime phase and the RAF attended the air phase without stamping their feet and moaning about going over areas that they had already covered earlier in their career. It was undoubtedly beneficial for everybody to attend the same course and be taught the same thing at the same time, as well as learning from the experience of your colleagues from the other services. The RLC continued to push back hard on this proposal and once again the idea was shelved.

Some years earlier a working group had paid some scientists to come up with a system for enabling near misses and narrowly avoided accidents to be reported confidentially without any recourse to the individual concerned. The system was similar in process to one that had been in existence in the RAF for many years and one that had proven to be extremely successful.

The EOD Confidential Hazard Occurrence System (ECHOS) was introduced in the early 2000s but not a single report had ever been raised. I was given the job of re-energising the system and in doing so I had meetings with the scientists who would be monitoring the results.

It turned out from my initial meeting that the MoD had been paying this firm to record and collate all the data that had been coming in and produce reports.

Of course, there had been no data and therefore no reports to compile but the company had continued to collect the payments and nobody had questioned the lack of data or reports. I told them that I would be running a twelve-month trial and if nothing was being produced or achieved I would be closing it down and therefore stopping the payments. Following on from that meeting I produced new reporting forms, instructions for completion and posters to advertise the existence of the process. I travelled all around the country to publicise the system and hoped that it would start to get used, although I was still sceptical. The RN already had a system and so did the RAF, and for the Army the idea of somebody doing something wrong and not getting punished for it was an alien concept. Twelve months later the coordinating company had not received a single report and as such the system was closed down.

When the head of JEODS changed over, the new incumbent decided that he was going to visit the Joint Force EOD Group in Afghanistan and decided to take me and a Royal Navy staff officer along with him for company and to reinforce the Joint Nature of JEODS to the EOD Group. The trip was fairly uneventful but very busy as we visited both Kandahar and Camp Bastion during our few days on the ground. At Camp Bastion one of the RLC EOD teams briefed us on a task that they had just carried out on a large air-dropped weapon (there were no RAF teams in theatre at this time). They explained how they could not clearly identify the bomb that was less than 30m from a remote bridge crossing and decided to revert to 'first principles'; covering it in plastic explosive and retreating to a safe distance to detonate it. The resultant explosion demolished the remote bridge and did very little, I imagine, to influence the hearts and minds campaign. They showed me photographs of the bomb and I immediately identified it as an American Mk 82, 500lb bomb; a weapon I had seen on many occasions during my time in Kosovo and whilst exercising with the USAF. I asked why they had not either towed the bomb to a location away from the bridge or attempted a deflagration technique. They gave me a puzzled look and told me that they were the operators on the ground and that I did not understand. It was another example of why all EOD operators should do the same course and be given the same information.

The branch received an invitation to a NATO meeting in Brussels and as several of us had key roles in the development of NATO procedures and publications we decided to have an office push to Brussels. One of the Army guys in the office decided that as RAF officers were rubbish with maps he would do all the organisation and co-ordination for the visit. We would be travelling on Eurostar and staying in the Belgian Military Officers Club in the centre of Brussels, which was where the meetings would be taking place. The event came around quickly and off we went on the train from Salisbury to Waterloo station in London, where we caught the Eurostar. A few hours later as we pulled into Brussels station our colleague told us it was time to get off the train and we followed his instructions and proceeded out of the station and down the main street. After ten minutes of dragging our suitcases we began to question if we were going in the right direction and if so how long it would be before we got to our accommodation. We stopped on a main junction to get our bearings and realised that we had no idea where we were and ended up hailing a taxi to take us to the accommodation, which was a good twenty-minute drive away.

There are two Eurostar stations in Brussels and we had got off at the wrong one. RAF officers might be rubbish with maps but it appears that Army officers are rubbish at everything.

Once the meetings commenced they took the usual path of the majority of NATO meetings and events with the UK, USA, Canada, France and the Netherlands playing key roles and doing all the work while the other nations either didn't turn up, went for a walk around town or watched DVDs on their laptops. The evenings were taken up with social events, sightseeing and visiting the bars in Brussels, of which there are many.

The Navy and the RLC had, for many years, been carrying out IED support to the Special Forces using a set of techniques and procedures know as assault IED. I was tasked by the head of JEODS to visit one of their training weeks to make sure that, in the brave new world of training authorisation and validation, everything was above board and being carried out in accordance with the correct training documentation and processes.

I drove to the training location and was met by the senior ammo techs who were delivering the training. They showed me around the training estate and admin facilities and we then went to observe some of the training scenarios. The training was excellent and very realistic, with each evolution being critiqued and debriefed by highly knowledgeable and experienced personnel. I had a fantastic week watching RN and RLC personnel operating at the top of their game.

As the week progressed I started to delve into the less appealing side of the training process and asked to see the training syllabi and lesson plans, whereupon I was met with a stony silence and a look of disdain. I was told that all the instructors were very experienced and knowledgeable individuals and that they just taught it by recalling their experiences. We then had a discussion covering issues such as how did we ensure that everybody got taught the same? How did we ensure that all pertinent information was passed on? How did we ensure that everybody was tested in the same way?

I was told that it had never been an issue before and nobody understood why I was raising such issues. I explained that the training process was defined in higher levels of documentation and that the process needed to be documented and recorded properly to ensure continuity and completeness and to stand up to any scrutiny that would follow on from any accidents or incidents.

They saw my point of view and promised to have the relevant paperwork drawn up and ready for publication in time for the next assault IED training event in six months' time. Six months later a colleague from JEODS and myself travelled to a different training establishment to watch another series of training events. We arrived on location, were met by a different group of senior ammo techs and we proposed to start the visit off with a proposed run through the newly developed training documentation.

My request was met with another stony silence and another look of disdain. The same conversation I had had six months earlier was carried out again but with a different group of individuals. At this point I made my feelings known and informed them that I would be writing formally to their chain of command requesting the appropriate documentation was put in place at the earliest opportunity. It still hadn't been by the time I left the job.

As we were based at HQ Land but were part of the MoD we did not carry out any HQ Land duties until one day one of the HQ Land officers took exception to this and suggested that we played our part in routine life at Wilton. Despite the protests from us all, and particularly the Navy and RAF members of the branch, we were told to bite the bullet and take our turn on the station duty officer roster. It came around to my turn and I walked over to the HQ Land building for the brief and handover, only to find that the off-going officer had forgotten to turn up for it. After several phone calls he was located and came running over to the main building.

He started talking in some strange Army language and kept referring to 'Johnny' in the swamp as my main point of contact. I stopped him and asked who Johnny in the swamp was? He looked at me in amazement and told me that it was unbelievable that someone who worked in Land HQ did not know who Johnny in the swamp was. I explained that I was an MoD staff officer and not from HQ Land, so he apologised and went on to explain that Johnny in the swamp was an Army ops officer in the operations cell who was the main point of contact for all issues. I slept in the duty bunk and all evening had a procession of phone calls and signal requests for HQ Land issues. On receiving the request, I looked through the HQ Land directory and called out the most appropriate person to deal with it as per the instructions. This was the sort of task that the RAF employed airmen for and seemed a complete overkill. I finished the duty and on my post-duty report highlighted my main concern that as a non-Army, non-Land HQ officer I was unfamiliar with the workings of Land HQ and therefore to carry out this duty was not efficient. Soon after my comments were made all RAF and Navy MoD staff officers were taken off the roster.

After a couple of years at JEODS I started to look around for my next job and without any shadow of a doubt the one I really wanted was that of OC 5131 (BD) Squadron. I made some enquiries and arranged to travel to RAF Wittering to have a chat with the wing commander that 5131 (BD) Squadron worked under to plead my case and try to secure the job. In my mind the timing was right as the current OC 5131 (BD) Squadron and I were due to move around the same time and I was the best qualified person for the job. I was EOD qualified and had done a tour on 5131 (BD) Squadron as a flight commander, a tour in the EOD Role Office, a tour in the MoD and two operational tours. Following on from my chat with the wing commander I spoke to the manning desk officer and he said he saw no reason why I should not get the job. My previous experiences with the manning people had led me not to take anything for granted but I was extremely hopeful that the move would come off, giving me not only the job I most wanted to do in the RAF but also the opportunity to move back home with the family.

The manning desk officer who said he saw no reason for me not to get the job was promoted and posted before I even got a whiff of a posting notice, so once again I became nervous that any agreement would be lost during the desk officer handover.

As an aside, in my ten years as a squadron leader there were a total of nine different desk officers who were supposed to be looking after my career. They never seemed to stay in post long enough to provide any continuity or stability and every one of them got moved on promotion. Despite the numerous denials from the organisation, I do not think it a coincidence when nine desk officers in a row get the manning job and then get promoted within eighteen months.

I called the newest incumbent to stake my claim and soon after that I went on holiday in the summer still not knowing where my next posting was going to be but still hopeful that I would get the OC 5131 (BD) Squadron job. I got off the aircraft in Orlando and turned on my phone to notice a text from the desk officer; I nervously opened the text to discover that my posting to Wittering as OC 5131 (BD) Squadron had been confirmed for later that year. I was absolutely ecstatic at the news and grateful to the desk officer for making it happen and letting me know. This was the type of service I had expected from the career managing desk officers but sadly this was the only one who met my expectations.

Once back from holiday it was time to start tying up the loose ends and preparing my handover brief for my replacement. Once the handover was completed it was time to pack up my room and move back home in preparation for taking over my new job.

Chapter 19

5131 (Bomb Disposal) Squadron (3)

I arrived at Wittering for my handover in the couple of weeks running up to Christmas. Timing wise it was good as the pace of work was slowing down in preparation for the Christmas break, so we could concentrate fully on the handover process without too many distractions. Having previously been on the squadron and having worked in the Role Office the handover was pretty easy as organisationally not a great deal had changed and we could just concentrate on new and current issues, of which there were many.

After the handover was completed and my predecessor had left I was fortunate enough to be invited to attend three arrivals interviews; one with my wing commander, one with the station commander and then surprisingly another with one of my flight commanders, who told me exactly what he needed from me in order for him to get promoted! Bizarre, but I suppose it takes all sorts.

The squadron were still playing a full and vital part in the provision of Military Support to the Civil Powers (MACP) and had two teams on call 24/7 to provide Improvised Explosive Device Disposal (IEDD) and Conventional Munitions Disposal (CMD) cover.

The provision of these teams was very time-consuming in terms of initial training, continuation training and time on duty, but it was the bread and butter of our task and was key in keeping us current and relevant. Historically, IEDD call outs average about one per month, with CMD call outs averaging around one per week.

The squadron still had a team in Iraq but that particular operation was in its final throes and the process of drawing down the troop numbers had already commenced. However, as the new squadron boss I considered it worthwhile to go to Basrah to visit the team and ensure that all was still well. On arrival, I was met by the RAF team and shown around the camp area. A great deal had changed since I was last there and the majority of personnel on the base were working hard to pack up and return any kit that was deemed surplus to requirements, and very few personnel actually operated outside of the airfield perimeter.

The Royal Engineers, who were in charge of the EOD Group, had already started to make and enforce some crazy rules, probably due to the boredom of running an EOD group that wasn't doing much EOD. The two daftest rules they were enforcing were the 'no sunbathing rule', even though every group had its own privacy behind concrete barriers, and the no civilian clothing except for regimental tracksuits rule, which was OK for the Royal Engineers but not so for the RAF and Navy personnel in the group. No self-respecting RAF armourer or Royal Navy diver was going to be seen dead in a Royal Engineer regimental tracksuit, so they had to wear their uniform 24/7. After my fleeting visit to Basrah it was time to fly back to the UK and work on which direction the squadron should be heading in the post-Iraq era.

My first job, however, was a lot closer to home in dealing with RAF EOD continuation training problems. Over the previous few years this training had developed into an extension of the initial EOD training courses and did not take into account that it was intended for already qualified and experienced operators.

There had been many instances of the squadron having very few EOD operators who were authorised to carry out tasks and duties, and they were constantly complaining about an inability to complete all their tasks. This was because people had failed the internal continuation course, making them unavailable for operational tasking, and had quickly developed into a clearly unsatisfactory situation. The issues, however, were down to the squadron internal continuation training programme and it was essentially a self-generated problem.

I booked myself onto the first available course with a view to getting myself authorised and current, and to assess where it was going wrong. After two weeks of refresher training I determined that it was clearly a good course but needed a radical rehash to make it more relevant to EOD operators who were already qualified and experienced.

Perhaps the best example of where it had lost its way was with the training modules for teaching teams how to carry out cluster munition disposal, something you will recall we used to be very good at due to our initial training, refresher training and experience on US ranges and on operations in Kosovo.

First of all, a classroom module was delivered that went through the theory of the disposal techniques, followed by a scenario-based event in the training compound using dummy explosives. Following on from that came a scenario out on the range using dummy explosives and then one on the final exercise using live explosives. I questioned as to why we were teaching in this way rather than just a quick refresh on techniques followed by a live explosive scenario out on the range. After all, the previous week all these operators would have been out and about in the UK or on operations carrying out real-time disposal.

At the end of the two-week course it was obvious that changes needed be made to make it shorter and more focused. I tasked the instructors with redesigning the course to make it a refresher, not for detailed instruction, and to reduce the training time to one week. The target was to turn out safe and competent EOD operators. In parallel to the redesign work I lobbied the EOD Role Office to get them to provisionally agree the changes we were proposing and set a very ambitious timeline in which to complete the work.

After a couple of weeks, I was summoned back to the Training Flight, where the instructors briefed me on their proposed changes to the course but disappointingly they stated they could only get the course length down to seven days and not the five I had asked for.

I was adamant that the five-day package was achievable so we spent the entire afternoon going through each and every module and looking at if and how we could reduce them. After a great deal of discussion and debate, often heated, we trimmed the modules sufficiently to allow it to be delivered in five days. The EOD Role Office had already agreed in principle to what we were proposing and we decided that the next course in a couple of weeks' time would be run in the new and revised format to check its suitability. It went well with all operators overjoyed at the reduced time taken to complete the refresher training and at the more grown up approach to the training.

RAF EOD had achieved a great deal in taking part in operations as part of the Joint Service EOD Group. Our taking part, and our performance, in both Kosovo and Iraq had giving us a large amount of kudos and had also helped develop a large operational experience level right across the squadron. With the operation in Iraq winding down and the operation in Afghanistan ramping up it was going to be vital for us to secure a place at the table when it came to Afghanistan operations to maintain that experience and for RAF EOD to remain relevant. With the full blessing of the hierarchy at Air Command, I spent the next few months lobbying hard with my contacts in the Army to get RAF EOD teams and commanders into the task force that was being reprofiled to meet with the nature and pace of operations in Afghanistan.

The Royal Engineers, as ever, were struggling with manpower and this was presenting the best opportunity to use RAF personnel to fill the void. The squadron WO and I travelled to Engineer HQ and the Engineer EOD HQ at Wimbish, where we met several of my previous contacts through my time in Kosovo, Iraq and JEODS and this made the whole process of putting my case forward a lot easier. As they already knew me and trusted me I did not have to go through the process of justifying my existence to them and we were able to very quickly cut to the chase and determine what jobs needed filling and how the RAF could help.

The pre-deployment process for this type of operation was going to be lengthy and we started out by identifying what training was going to be needed and how best to deliver it. It was decided that the training would be delivered at Wimbish and that the RAF personnel involved, once selected, would pretty much operate from there for the next six months prior to deploying on a six-month tour of duty in Afghanistan. This in itself caused the first conflict of interest as we explained that while the REs would be operating from their home base, the RAF personnel would not. Therefore, the training programme needed to be short and compact rather than long and drawn out to avoid them being away from their home base, and more importantly their family, any longer than necessary. This course of action was agreed and we returned to Wittering to set about the task of identifying the personnel to go on the first push.

As ever in these situations there was no shortage of volunteers for this venture and to write another exciting chapter for RAF EOD. After the operational experiences gained on previous EOD operational tours the squadron personnel were keen to build on them and help to keep RAF EOD at the forefront of the capability.

We had not been back at Wittering for long when I received a call from the REs stating that they were now short of an ops officer and asked if we had someone who could fill the role. This was another outstanding opportunity for the RAF to fill a key role in the EOD Group and one of the flight commanders volunteered without hesitation. This also presented us with an outstanding opportunity to have chain of command top cover for the guys who were going out as EOD teams during both the training and operational phases. We selected an EOD commander/ops officer, a four-man team for the operation and a four-man reserve team who would cover for any fall downs in the first team and then deploy on the second rotation after the first six months.

Just as we were completing the selection and nomination of personnel, the Army had identified an urgent need for an EOD-focused intelligence officer in the HQ in Afghanistan in the next few weeks and asked if we could help. Another of the squadron flight commanders volunteered to fill this post and, having received some very abbreviated pre-deployment training (PDT), he moved at short notice to fill the post. In hindsight, we should have resisted this approach as it was leaving us thin on the ground on the squadron and was putting somebody into an area that was outside his specialisation (something the Army do regularly but not so much the RAF). He performed well, enjoyed the experience and having completed his six-month tour he came back with a wealth of knowledge that he put to good use, further developing personnel on the squadron for joint operations.

The nine personnel deployed to Wimbish to meet their RE colleagues and to commence the PDT that would see them being trained in all EOD and infantry disciplines needed to operate on the front line in Afghanistan. Once they had gone through all the administrative tasks and taking over their accommodation, they started training in earnest and in the only way the REs knew how. They were introduced to some rather large logs and went on a 5-mile log run with the rest of the group. Not the greatest introduction to your next six months of PDT as they had expected a gradual increase in physical activity, not going balls out from the start. In fairness, not many of the REs were prepared for this physically demanding start to the training either and there were many injuries suffered during that run and in the rest of the first week's physical activities.

In most circumstances, the extent and amount of injuries would have prompted a rethink of training methods and intensity but not on this occasion and the training got harder and more intensive to the extent that morale was plummeting at an astonishing rate and it was obvious that something needed to be done.

This extreme physical exercise, coupled with the ridiculously basic level of EOD training being delivered as part of the PDT, prompted the RAF EOD commander and the team SNCOs to question the PDT programme and the necessity of them being at Wimbish for five days a week for the full six months. Some days they were left sitting around for hours on end whilst RE-specific training was carried out and, in the evenings, when the REs went home to their families, the nine RAF personnel were left kicking their heels in sparse accommodation with nothing to do and nowhere to go. They spoke to one of the RE ops officers, who just said they would have to 'suck-it-up' and stop moaning. This feedback prompted me and the squadron WO to arrange another visit to Wimbish to have a meeting with the regiment CO and his command team to work out a more sensible approach to the PDT.

As I expected, he had not been informed of the ongoing worsening situation with morale and the fact that the RAF personnel were left kicking their heels for hours on end, and he was very understanding of the need to keep my guys happy. We agreed to look at the six-month PDT package and decide on which elements were essential, desirable or not required from an RAF point of view and take it from there. This review produced a far more palatable training schedule for the RAF teams and gave them more time to carry out their own prep and spend time with their families before proceeding on what was undoubtedly going to be a very arduous, stressful and dangerous tour of duty.

Now that this hurdle had been overcome, the next hurdle was to get the RAF Regiment training system to acknowledge that much of the all-arms or infantry-type training the teams were getting at Wimbish was equivalent to, if not better than, that delivered by the RAF in the Common Core Skills (CCS) packages. Again, this assurance was essential in order to ensure that none of the 5131 (BD) Squadron personnel had to do any training package twice just to satisfy the egos of either the Army or the RAF Regiment. Believe it or not it took several months of work to get this assurance but we managed in the end and developed a strategy for coping with this issue, not just for this turn of the handle but for all future teams preparing to go to Afghanistan as part of the Joint EOD Group.

As the training progressed the team were becoming more and more competent in performing infantry skills alongside their already high level of EOD skills and they quickly became the focus of attention for the hierarchy of the RAF. We had RAF armourers and engineers who were going out to Afghanistan to operate well outside the base security areas as part of Joint EOD Task Force.

I seized the opportunity to further enhance and publicise the case for RAF EOD and arranged several media days with the help of the command team and the media communications people at RAF Wittering. We had TV and radio coverage and articles published in local newspapers and various magazines. The appetite for RAF EOD had never been higher.

The culmination of the PDT saw all brigade elements taking part in a combined exercise on Salisbury Plain and an invitation was sent to a selection of senior command chain members to attend the event to see how their personnel had developed and progressed during the process. I was exceptionally pleased that my wing commander and the new station commander (only a couple of days into his new job) decided to attend with me to see how the guys had been getting on and to meet them and hear their stories. Even more pleasing was that on the VIP day our two-star officer from Air Command also took the opportunity to come along and even shared a helicopter with the senior Army officers attending the event. The kudos and reputation of RAF EOD was climbing higher and higher by the day, and whilst I felt extremely proud as the squadron boss in getting us into this position I was more proud of the guys who had endured the intense and arduous training and come out of it with flying colours. From here on in they were affectionately known as my 'A Team'.

Once these first five personnel had deployed to Afghanistan the cycle from then on became ongoing, with teams being nominated and trained in rotation.

The RLC were now struggling to provide high-threat (HT) IED operators for the operation and again I sensed another opportunity to push the RAF into another, as yet, previously unexplored area. I canvassed the IED operators on the squadron to gauge the level of interest in tackling the fearsome HT IED course. There was keen interest, particularly among the more experienced operators, so again with the blessing of the hierarchy I put forward a name for the HT course. The individual would effectively live and breathe IED for the next eighteen months, with several courses to do.

Time was now flying by and the first team and the commander were due back from Afghanistan having completed a very successful and arduous tour of duty. They had performed extremely well, had carried out numerous tasks and, more importantly, had come back unharmed. Their medals had been sent to Wimbish and the proposal from the Army was that they would be presented by a senior Army officer at a ceremony to be arranged the following month. I fed this information through the RAF hierarchy, during which the Air Command two-star who had attended the exercise at Salisbury Plain said, 'Over my dead body, they are RAF personnel and I will present them with their medals.' Who was I to argue? I passed the information to the Army that the RAF personnel would be getting their medals presented by our two-star and arranged for them to be collected from Wimbish and taken to High Wycombe.

On the day in question we travelled to High Wycombe, got changed into our number one home dress and attended a very private and poignant medal ceremony in the officers' mess. In attendance was the two-star, his staff officer, the five recipients, the squadron WO and me. After the presentation, the two-star had arranged for us all to have lunch together at a reserved table in the officers' mess dining room, finishing the day off in style and making all the medal recipients feel very special, which of course they were.

After several months, and a few attempts, we eventually got somebody through the HT IED course and set another RAF milestone as he became the first non-RLC person to pass the course. He deployed with his RAF assistant and a team configured of other specialists at the same time as we had other, none HT teams, operating in Afghanistan.

Back on the squadron, we had a lot of EOD assistants volunteering for operational tours in Afghanistan and it soon became apparent that the amount of team leaders we were generating would never match the numbers of volunteer assistants. We canvassed opinion as to the willingness of the Army to accept RAF assistants and the desire of the RAF personnel to act as assistants for Army team leaders and to my surprise, but with immense pride, they were all more than willing to do so. Over the peak operational years of the campaign we provided a number of assistants to Army teams and they all came back safely having undergone some harrowing and horrific experiences but had also learned a huge amount from their tours and gained more kudos for the RAF. In parallel we also continued to put more people through the high-threat IED course but only succeeded in generating one more HT IED operator.

I recall that at one time we had ten personnel from 5131 (BD) Squadron in the Joint EOD Group. Thankfully they all came back unharmed and one of the high-threat operators was awarded the Queen's Gallantry Medal (QGM) for his actions during his tour of duty.

At the end of this particular tour of duty an EOD Group medal presentation was held at Woodbridge, to which I received an invite along with the wing commander and the squadron WO. The whole of the EOD Group was at this presentation but it was exceptionally memorable and poignant for me as bringing up the rear of the parade as they marched on to the parade square were several of those personnel who had been wounded during that tour. It was heart-wrenching to see young soldiers in the prime of their life in wheelchairs and on crutches having suffered unimaginable injuries. Despite their horrific injuries they still stood or sat to attention in their uniform as they were presented with their medals and displayed remarkable fortitude and cheeriness.

The constant political and tri-service infighting was probably the main feature of my time as OC 5131 (BD) Squadron. But at the end of that tour we showed that as an organisation we could mix it with the very best and were more than able and capable of operating way outside our comfort zone. Despite the interest shown by the hierarchy at that stage it would soon wane again and RAF EOD would once again become something that nobody really wanted or needed. Until they needed it!

As the shortage of EOD operators in the Army became ever more acute, the Army decided to open up the EOD course to all Army personnel subject to them passing an aptitude test. They produced a defence notice explaining the process but forgot to mention that it was only meant for the Army.

As a result of this oversight, a couple of RAF personnel who were not from the Armament or Engineer specialisation (one air loadmaster and one RAF Regiment officer) applied, were accepted and were loaded onto the course by the RAF manning personnel. Through my contacts at the Defence EOD School I got wind of this development and called the EOD Role Office to find out what was going on. I explained that the RAF didn't have a shortage of operators and therefore there was no need to open up the RAF places to non-weapons specialists. I was told by the EOD Role Office that the individuals had been told that they were on the course and that there was no way of stopping them now. The armament knowledge and familiarisation with aircraft weapon systems was always a key factor in passing the EOD course and opening it up to the rest of the RAF would have been damaging to the morale of the weapons trade as a whole, but particularly to the EOD operators on the squadron.

I called Air Command to express my concerns and after a while they agreed with me and asked me to contact the relevant people to get them taken off the course. I spoke to the EOD Role Office again and explained to them the wishes of the Air Command group captain, to which they said that there wasn't much they could do.

I suggested that they had two options: option one was to get them taken off the course, with option two being to phone the group captain and explain why they had let it get this far and why they couldn't change it. They opted for option one.

In parallel, and as highlighted during my time at Salisbury in JEODS, there was another push to get the RLC operators the same qualification as all other EOD operators but without them having to do the full course. They persevered with the rationale that they were ammo techs and therefore did not need to do many of the modules on the DEODS course as they knew everything and if in doubt they would refer to first principles. What this actually meant nobody was quite sure but the RAF and Navy personnel knew all about air and maritime weapons respectively and still had to do those modules, however they just got on with it.

I received a phone call one day asking me to develop an air-dropped weapon phase for the RLC that would give them the knowledge usually attained on the DEODS course. I got the Training Flight to do a quick calculation as to how long it would take and they came up with a very reasonable, or so I thought, one-week course. I passed the information back and was told that a week was far too long and that we should be looking at something closer to two days. I told Air Command that delivering a two-day course was insufficient to pick up all the training objectives and that I considered anything less than five days was at best dangerous and at worst an insult to all those who had done the course properly. This point was made in an even firmer manner when I was told that the course would be delivered in a classroom with no practical tests and no examinations. After several days of discussion, I lost the battle and I was ordered to deliver all the training objectives to two classes of RLC EOD team leaders and that the sessions would take no longer than two days and would be run consecutively.

On day one of the first course I attended the welcome brief to greet the students to 5131 (BD) Squadron and to explain the outline for the course. I was outraged by the attitude and general demeanour of the majority of the students, who continued with the pre-course misconception that they knew everything and did not need to be there. I did not expect this type of attitude from a group of senior and commissioned personnel but unfortunately the no test and no exam restraints placed on my training team allowed the students to pay lip service to the course, get the tick in the box they needed and go out into the world being hopelessly prepared but not wanting to admit it. This course became known as the 'RLC Patch Course' but in reality it was little more than a sticking plaster on a gaping wound.

Another burning issue during my time as OC 5131 (BD) Squadron was the continued occupation and permanent manning of several former air weapon ranges (outsites). These outsites were spread around the UK and had a permanent staff with a mix of service personnel parented by RAF Wittering and civilian staff recruited from the local community as EOD searcher/drivers. RAF EOD had been working on these sites for many years and whilst steady progress was made on them all there was no end in sight, especially if the end state was the complete clearance and safety certification of each location.

There was very little unexploded ordnance being found on any of the sites but there was a significant amount of scrap metal from exploded ordnance. I decided that it was not cost-effective in terms of either manpower, time or equipment to continue manning and clearing these sites, so I made proposals to scale down the operations with a view to withdrawing from them at the earliest opportunity. A couple of the sites would be relatively easy to scale down and close but there would be three in particular that would take more time and work to achieve my aim.

We closed the sites at Chilmark and Donna Nook within a few months and stopped clearance on the site at Theddlethorpe. We did, however, keep the range open at Theddlethorpe as it was a convenient and self-managed range that we could continue to use for both training and for the disposal of recovered items of ordnance from MACP tasks.

The easy part done, next I looked at the three remaining sites of Braid Fell, Goswick Sands and Cowden and started to develop a plan for their closure. None of these sites were going to be easy to scale down and close but for very different reasons. Braid Fell needed to be returned to its original condition (allegedly) and had some very strong personalities working on it; Goswick Sands was close to a popular tourist destination and was in the constituency of a long serving Lib Dem politician; and Cowden was the most recently used site and suffered from extensive coastal erosion. In addition to all of the problems listed above, we would need to carry out a full trade union (TU) consultation for each site as the proposals would result in the loss of jobs for the civilian staff.

Braid Fell was an old test range on the outskirts of Stranraer that had been used extensively for all kinds of weapon testing between 1944 and 2000. According to everyone I spoke to the rumour was that in order to hand the site back to its owner it needed to be returned to its original condition. I first visited the site in the early days of my tenure as squadron boss and it then became obvious to me that returning the site to how it once was would be an impossible task. While we could continue to search the deserted moorland with metal detectors and dig out scrap metal for tens, if not hundreds, of years, there were areas that had been turned into swampland and there was no way of reversing that process.

I arranged to have a meeting with the landowner's representative to discuss the options and found that they had never even mentioned returning the land to its original condition. All they wanted was an assurance that if anything suspicious was ever found on the land after we left that we would return to clear it and that they would never be held responsible for any costs or liability if anybody was ever injured by an item of ordnance found there. This all seemed perfectly reasonable and we agreed to detail those requests in any documentation that was produced as part of the process.

The TU demanded a meeting on site to discuss all options and future employment possibilities for the civilian staff. Again, I had no problem with meeting this request but was a bit peeved when they insisted that we had the meeting early on a Monday morning. We travelled up on the Sunday and were then told that we (the RAF) had to pay for a meeting room in a local hotel in which the TU could hold their meeting with the staff. Again, I agreed to this proposal and then the TU rep told me that we could not be present at the meeting but had to sit around in the hotel foyer until they were ready to let us in and hear our proposal. So here I was hundreds of miles from home sitting in a hotel foyer waiting to be allowed into a room that I had paid to hire. Eventually we were allowed in and explained our proposal, which was agreed in principle subject to a full TU consultation paper being written and a promise that the civilian staff would be properly looked after during and after the closure announcement.

After about six months of the consultation paper going backwards and forwards to make minor amendments the proposal was signed off and a date agreed for the closure of the site. A couple of weeks after closure we received a call through the MACP process to attend the site at Braid Fell as a suspicious item had been found. It was nothing of interest and was probably somebody trying to make a point and make us drive six hours each way to attend the incident. We did as agreed in the closure documentation and never got called back after that.

It was now time to switch my attention to the site at Goswick Sands, which was a beach site just south of Berwick-upon-Tweed and north of Holy Island. Several large items of live ordnance had been discovered there over the previous years but all of them had been located using highly technical metal detection techniques and heavy-duty excavation. The local MP for the region had taken a keen interest in the site as it was high profile, close to tourist attractions and he had been fed some mistruths by several personnel. He decided to focus on making us keep the site open. By keeping it open he was securing some local jobs, a worthy cause, but at the same time he was diverting military manpower that was much needed on deployed operations rather than looking for scrap metal on a beach in Northumberland.

His concerns become so over the top that I agreed to meet him and discuss them with him as well as giving him a tour of the entire site. Due to the distance from RAF Wittering, I drove up the day before the visit and stayed overnight in service accommodation at RAF Boulmer and drove up to the site the following day. On the day in question I met the MP along with the service and civilian members of staff who permanently manned the site. We discussed all issues surrounding infrastructure, equipment and manning and then set out for a drive around the entire site area.

As we drove across the beach, the permanent staff were constantly pointing out items on the beach and telling the MP that these were the items of ordnance that they were encountering on a daily basis. He turned to me and expressed his concerns that these highly dangerous items should not be left unattended and should be dealt with at the earliest opportunity, and that it was obvious that the site should remain manned for the foreseeable future.

At this point I asked the team to drive to several of the items and at each stop we would get out of the vehicle and explain to the MP what it was that we were looking at. At each and every stop I explained to him that what we were looking at was in fact scrap metal that posed no threat to anybody and that items of ordnance rising to the surface was a very rare occurrence. Any that did appear were called in to the local police, who would call out disposal teams through the Joint Service EOD Ops Centre.

The team then proceeded to tell him that having a permanent team on site meant that the local police could call out its members rather than go through the Joint Ops Centre. I pointed out that the local team were not on duty at evenings or weekends and did not hold the relevant items of explosives to deal with all eventualities. Therefore they could not provide an appropriate response to any items that were called in.

He listened to my explanation and saw my point of view, and he claimed to be coming around to my way of thinking. Feeling happy with myself, I bade him goodbye and set off on the five-hour drive back to Wittering.

A few days later my attention was brought to an article in a Northeast local newspaper in which the MP was claiming that the RAF was not fulfilling its duty of care as we were proposing to leave the site with dangerous ordnance lying all over the beach. Sometimes you just wonder why you bother!

The Goswick Sands closure and the process of closing down the final site at Cowden would both rumble on for some time and would follow me on into the next chapter.

With the squadron commitment to operations in Afghanistan and the rapidly changing training courses, life was extremely busy and seldom did you have time to draw breath. That commitment and pace of life coupled with the rapid turnover of flight commanders (in the three flight commander posts on the squadron, I had eight incumbents in two and a half years) led me to request a tour extension from two to three years. My request was approved and supported by both the wing commander and the station commander and agreed with the desk officer. It was a fantastic result for me as it was more time in the best job in the world and more time living at home with the family.

The increase in RAF EOD involvement in all things bomb disposal both at home and abroad encouraged me to dust off and resubmit one of my predecessors' pieces of work to get a squadron standard awarded to 5131 (BD) Squadron.

A standard was historically awarded by the Queen to flying squadrons and also to RAF Regiment squadrons as those two entities were deemed to be at the fighting end of the service's capability. As the flying squadrons were now doing their fighting from adjacent countries and at 20,000ft plus and the RAF Regiment were operating on and in the localised vicinity of main operating bases, it seemed logical that as 5131 (BD) Squadron were operating well ahead of the front line now was a good time to resubmit the work.

I redrafted the previous submission to include the detail of the Kosovo campaign, Iraq and Afghanistan and how 5131 (BD) Squadron were at the very forefront of war fighting capability, operating in some of the harshest and most unforgiving environments on earth. At the time of the submission we had numerous EOD operators and teams at the very cutting edge of the bomb disposal capability. Alas, the ivory towers could not see the irony of RAF EOD teams driving past RAF Regiment personnel on their way out of the base to carry out many arduous hours of technically demanding and dangerous disposal work. The submission was again rejected primarily because, up in the ivory towers, nobody could be bothered to challenge the status quo.

RAF bomb disposal was still flavour of the month and we were getting invites to take part in all sorts of displays and demonstrations at various locations around the country. On one such occasion we were supporting an RAF Regiment-led capability demonstration at RAF Waddington for the then Defence Secretary. We were there to provide an EOD demonstration as part of the event showcasing our part in operations in Afghanistan. The 'A' team from Afghanistan were always the display team but as we got more teams through the operational theatre we had more to choose from. As always, the display we put on was impressive, realistic and well received by the dignitaries viewing it. We had remote control vehicles and live explosives had been authorised, so every event went off with a bang and left a lasting impression on everybody who witnessed it.

It was during one of these displays that I received a call from a colleague, who informed me that he was being posted in to replace me in a couple of months' time. This came as a huge shock to me as I was still nine months away from my newly agreed posting point at the end of a three-year tour. I rang my wing commander, who sheepishly admitted that he had had a conversation with the manning desk officer about me being posted early but that nothing had been agreed. He rang me back a couple of hours later apologising for not speaking to me about it before it had been decided but the bottom line was that my replacement, my boss and my career manager had all had a conversation, the result of which was that I was to be posted to the EOD Role Office that was now part of the Arm Role Office at HQ Air Command. I was a little bit peeved, having had my tour extended and then cut short, but accepted that there were mitigating circumstances. That said, I couldn't help feeling that I had been pushed out once again. I went home, told the family and started planning for another beany tour living in the officers' mess at RAF High Wycombe.

Chapter 20

Explosive Ordnance Disposal (EOD) Role Office High Wycombe

I arrived at High Wycombe with my car packed to the gunnels with all of the essential stuff needed for living in the mess for a few years. TV, fridge microwave, pushbike and, most important of all, my PlayStation 3.

Towards the end of my time at Wittering there had been rumours that in the next round of defence cuts the RAF was looking to get rid of its EOD capability and on arrival at High Wycombe during my arrival brief this course of action was confirmed.

How ironic that as one of the most outspoken supporters of RAF EOD my next job would be to get rid of it. Or would it?

The EOD-supporting two-star officer who had attended the PDT VIP day at Salisbury Plain had moved on and the new two-star had very little time for, or interest in, RAF EOD. The same could be said for the one-star, the group captain and the wing commander, so I was definitely going to have my work cut out if I was going to save the capability from extinction. But with a knowledgeable team of EOD personnel in the EOD RO we would have to work fast and smart if we were going to save it.

The first step was for the wing commander to book an appointment with the two-star in which he would outline his plans and reasons for getting rid of RAF EOD and this would be my first opportunity to sow the seeds of doubt. The meeting went well but the two-star still seemed adamant that he was going to offer up the RAF EOD capability as a cost-saving measure and stated that the Army would cover the gap left by RAF EOD. As my parting shot I mentioned my vast experience of working with Army EOD and asked if he really wanted them to operate on airfields working around millions of pounds worth of aircraft.

I also questioned how, if we needed the RAF Regiment as air-minded infantry, we were happy to have non-air minded EOD teams? Seed of doubt sown, I waited for the fallout.

In the meantime, I had also been ploughing ahead with the paperwork and consultation documents for the closure of the Goswick Sands site. Out of the blue, the wing commander and I were summoned to see the Minister for the Armed Forces (MinAF) in London to explain our rationale behind closing the site. A bit of homework revealed that MinAF was a Lib Dem MP and was a close associate of the MP for the region in which the Goswick Sands site was situated. The latter had obviously put forward his objections to our proposal and had gained some support from MinAF. We attended the meeting and put forward our case based on the fact that we were not closing the site but we were altering the way in which we manned and monitored it. MinAF agreed that what we were proposing was a cost-effective and less manpower-intensive strategy for looking after the site, and authorised us to carry on with our plan. As a result of this outcome the local MP had one last card to play and organised a meeting for the numerous local action groups and concerned parties to be briefed on the proposal.

I agreed to travel to Goswick Sands and brief all parties in a village hall that had been booked by the MP and his team. I drove the eight hours to RAF Boulmer, again checked into my accommodation and turned up at the village hall in good time to set up the visual aids equipment ready to deliver my brief to the many interested and concerned locals. There were less than a dozen people at the briefing and that included me, the MP and his researcher and several members of the service and civilian staff from the site. Hardly the baying crowd I had been warned to expect.

Briefing delivered and difficult questions answered, I travelled back to Boulmer for the night and then set off for High Wycombe the following morning. Once back in the office, I completed the TU consultation document and site withdrawal proposal and after another few months of the documents going back and forth for minor tweaks it was all agreed and signed off.

The time had come for the annual budget rounds and the budget-saving proposal of deleting the RAF EOD capability came to a head once more. We now had a new group captain in charge of the Arm Role

Office and he came to see me one day and asked for my views. I gave him my thoughts and he said that we should not assume it was a done deal and asked me to write a paper on my proposals to keep the capability. Any proposal would have to be at worst cost neutral but any ideas that could be put forward that would protect the capability while also offering budget savings would be easier to justify and get through the scrutineers. The budget round passed without the need to go into battle to save the capability but all agreed that we should press ahead with the proposal as we would be able to staff it in good time for the following year's budget round when the deletion of the capability would surely come up again.

While all this was going on, the bombing campaign to get rid of Colonel Gaddafi in Libya had commenced and concluded, and several teams were being put together to fly to Libya to assist the new regime to clear up following on from an intensive air bombing campaign. We put forward a proposal that any team deployed to Libya should contain RAF air-dropped weapons experts, and indeed we highlighted that the RAF had a team who were on standby for such a requirement. We were told that they were not required at the moment but we should keep them on standby as things were developing very quickly.

On arrival at work one morning we had a message from 5131 (BD) Squadron to call them reference a telephone conversation that they had taken the previous night. An RLC Ammo Tech had called them from Libya seeking advice on how to identify air-dropped bombs and the fuzes they contained. Some of the assumptions made on the ground were at best rubbish and at worst extremely dangerous, so we left a message with 5131 (BD) Squadron that if the individual called again they should give him our number and get him to call us. At the same time, it was highlighted that the individual concerned had also been putting pictures and details on Facebook. The 'RLC Patch Course' had obviously done its job as we now had an ammo tech driving around Libya pretending he knew what he was talking about and trying all the time to get information from either Facebook or the real experts on 5131 (BD) Squadron.

After a few phone calls and discussions trying to find out how we got to such a situation, it turned out that some genius at the Air Warfare Centre had put a team together to look for some of the unexploded air-dropped weapons in order to gain intelligence for the defence contractors who had manufactured them. He was unaware that the RAF had such a capability and went to the Joint Service Ops Centre, who identified an RLC Ammo Tech to do the job, despite them being aware of the RAF capability. After much pushing to get the RAF team into the country it was decided that it was now too late to change things and the team were stood down.

It was now time to look at the closure or drawing down of the Cowden outsite and this was always going to be the hardest one of all of them to close. Due to coastal erosion, the cliffs on site were always collapsing and with every such occurrence a huge amount of ordnance was deposited on the beach. Most of the ordnance was exploded and therefore scrap metal but much of it had been buried in the cliffs for so long that it was difficult if not impossible to tell.

Once again, the local community had a lot of concerns over what we would continue to do after the site had closed and it was clear that the only way to allay these concerns was to deliver a briefing similar to the one I had delivered at Goswick Sands. Once briefed the locals were more onside as to the way we proposed to monitor the site in future and were content with our plan.

Back at High Wycombe the relevant paperwork was completed and was agreed and signed off in fairly short order. The speed of this action was mainly down to the fact that we had done numerous site proposals by now, so we had a framework to work from and were aware of all of the protocols and pitfalls.

The EOD capability proposal paper was nearing completion now and was ready for its first round of circulation to the hierarchy. It was based on an overall reduction in squadron manpower but closely linked to a reduction in task, improved training pass quotas and the squadron not carrying any dead, sick, dying or unqualified personnel in its manning figures. It passed its first round of circulation with a few minor amendments and it was now time to turn it into a budget proposal format ready for submission. After an extreme amount of back and forth staffing, the proposal was approved and the RAF EOD capability was saved.

There would be a lot of hard work ahead and none of it would be plain sailing, but at least the RAF would be retaining its EOD capability until the next time somebody wanted to save money based on something they knew nothing about.

A smaller and leaner EOD capability would be a less attractive employment opportunity to a lot of people, so I spoke to the manning desk officer (another different one) and explored the possibility of me returning to 5131 (BD) Squadron as the boss again to implement the changes suggested by the EOD paper. Nobody else had expressed an interest in the job so he told me that there was no reason that I should not get the job when it became available. Happy days!

The NATO TACEVAL regime was still running at this time but at a much slower pace than in previous years. I was offered the chance to go to Sicily as a Force Protection Command and Control evaluator for an evaluation of the E-3 AWACS force. As I had never been to Sicily I seized the opportunity and travelled to Palermo and then on to Trapani for the evaluation. The whole evaluation process was slow and uneventful, with the highlight of the trip being a day trip to the base of Mount Etna on one of the down days.

Meanwhile, the new wing commander in the Arm RO had decided that as the number of personnel in the office was shrinking he would combine all elements and specialisations into one open plan office. One member of the EOD Role Office had already been disestablished so it was just the two of us to move next door. There were other postings out of the office so I filled in for one of the other squadron leader arm posts for a short time until another person was posted in. It was a very interesting and busy time in the office with every day bringing a new and varied challenge.

My EOD partner in crime in the office was looking to secure a posting to somewhere closer to home and had identified a job that was becoming available. He phoned his career manager, who informed him that he could have the job if he wanted it but also told him that he would not be replaced in the Role Office as his post had been disestablished. He queried as to why it had been disestablished and was told that it was because the EOD capability was being got rid of. He corrected them on that fact and told them that the capability would be continuing but the career manager said that it was a done deal and that there was no way of reversing the manning disestablishment.

In a state of shock, he went to tell the wing commander, who looked like a rabbit caught in the headlights as he was told the news, but did nothing about it. The following day, I mentioned to the wing commander that if the WO post had been disestablished it was highly likely that mine could also have been binned. He said that that would never happen and not to worry about it!

Shortly after, I turned up for work and as I fired up my computer I noticed an email from the manning desk officer (yes you guessed it another different one). His email said that as my post had been disestablished and I had not been out of area for a long time he would be posting me to a secret location in the Middle East (SLME) for a six-month tour. I dashed straight to the wing commander's office as, in my view, two critical posts being lost in a very short space of time when RAF EOD needed continuity as it transformed would warrant some sort of reaction, but not here! It turned out that a logistics wing commander had restructured this floor of Air Command but had not kept up to date with what was going on with regards to the EOD capability.

He had to get rid of so many posts and had safeguarded the logistics ones at the expense of everything else. By the time this restructuring had taken place there would be more logisticians in the Arm Role Office than armourers. I walked across to the adjacent office block to have a face-to-face chat with the desk officer (the same one this time but it was only a day later).

He told me that I had only been OOA once and that was in 2003, so therefore it was my turn to go again. I pointed out that I had done OOA tours in Italy, the Falklands, Kosovo and Iraq, and I listed numerous colleagues who had not done half of what I had done. He reluctantly agreed with me but said that as my post was being disestablished he had to do something with me.

I mentioned his predecessor's agreement that I could go back to 5131 (BD) Squadron and that that job was now becoming available but he shrugged his shoulders and said I should start preparing for my OOA tour. As OOA tours go the one to which I was being assigned sounded interesting so I didn't want to push back too hard in case I ended up with something rubbish.

I agreed to go without kicking up a fuss but asked for a job at Wittering on my return as I would be in my last two years of service and it would enable me to live at home as I prepared to leave the RAF. There was one particular job that I asked for at Wittering and I outlined that from that job I could continue to monitor and shape the transformation of 5131 (BD) Squadron as some sort of dual-hatted pseudo EOD Role Office job.

I was told that I was not suitably qualified and experienced to carry out that role, which was a roundabout way of telling me I couldn't have it as the current incumbent didn't want to move.

I was more suitably qualified for the job than any of the previous four incumbents but sometimes you just have to accept that you are not going to win an argument. I was offered the job of OC 5001 Squadron, and whilst it was not in my area of specialisation it did offer me a good, punchy and high-profile job that was close to home. Not wishing to get done over whilst I was away, I requested a posting notification and a confirmation email to give me some sort of guarantee that my posting to 5001 Squadron was a done deal. I got the notifications I asked for and just had to hope that the desk officers did not change and break all agreements and promises, again.

The Arm Role Office was now going through massive changes with regard to manpower and responsibilities and having people posted out and not replaced was not going to help things. I did, however, still have a few months to tidy up the loose ends and pass over the remaining tasks to various people in order for them to provide some continuity. However, by the time all the PDT requirements for my OOA tour had been identified my few months would soon turn into a few weeks.

Nobody could give me an exact date for my flight to the SLME and trying to plan my PDT and some leave before going was more difficult than it should have been. I had a back stop date to arrive in SLME by and started to count back from there with a couple of weeks' leave, planning all my PDT to be complete by the start of that leave period. I needed to complete a week of RAF Regiment-led PDT and the course I needed was held at both High Wycombe and Wittering. It seemed like a relatively painless task to either do one at High Wycombe, where I was still living in the mess, or even better would be one at Wittering where I could live at home for a week. However, the only course available was at RAF Leeming and it ran immediately up to the start of my two weeks' leave. I booked myself on that course, cleared my desk and room at High Wycombe, moved home for the weekend and travelled up to Leeming.

The course was another catch all, tick in the box exercise that had little, if any, relevance to my posting.

Halfway through the course I got a call from manning saying that my back stop date had been brought forward by a week and that I would no longer be able to have two weeks' leave prior to deploying. After some debate over the phone and by email I was told that the SLME had been consulted and that they were adamant that I needed to arrive by the revised date. Throughout all this training and planning I was also told that I had to be Security DV and STRAP cleared (DV and STRAP clearance is for personnel who will have unrestricted access to top secret material) and that I needed to commence the process early as it could take up to sixty days to complete. I was told this with fewer than fifty days to go, so was already up against a seemingly impossible timeline. I managed to get my DV completed in around forty-five days and arranged to have my STRAP clearance done at RAF Wittering, thereby saving me a bit of travelling time.

Training at Leeming completed, briefings at PJHQ attended, Security clearance signed off and all associated preparation boxes ticked, it was home for a week's leave before travelling to Brize Norton to catch my flight.

As I was in limbo between High Wycombe and Wittering I then had difficulty getting service transport to take me to Brize Norton. High Wycombe would take me but I had to travel there to catch the transport; Wittering would not take me as I was not posted to them yet. The drive to High Wycombe would take longer than the drive to Brize Norton so in the end my wife drove me to catch my flight. The same problem would occur during my R&R.

Chapter 21

Secret Location Middle East (SLME)

After an eight-hour flight, I arrived at SLME, which was to be my home for the next six months. My new job was titled Chief of Staff Support (COS Spt) for 906 Expeditionary Air Wing (EAW) and it basically meant that I was in charge of pretty much everything that did not fall into the movements, infrastructure or RAF Regiment brackets. The primary function of the EAW was to support the Middle East airbridge, support the removal of armoured vehicles from Afghanistan and provide support to exercising UK fast jet squadrons. It was a very diverse and demanding mission, especially as during my time in SLME we had three visiting fast jet squadrons spread over the six-month period.

Within minutes of getting off the aircraft my predecessor took me to an infrastructure siting board meeting to discuss the potential plans for a future infrastructure project. My bags were still in the back of the car as we stood in the 30 degrees + heat having just endured an overnight flight and I was flagging to say the least. All I really wanted to do was find my accommodation, unpack my bags, have a shower and grab a couple of hours' sleep. After a whistle-stop three-day handover my predecessor left and I was now alone to face my new and somewhat daunting challenge.

During my handover period, I raised the question as to why my request to have my arrival delayed by a week had been turned down. I was told that nobody from manning had ever contacted them about delaying my arrival and a short delay would not have been a problem. It was obviously the easy option for manning to just turn my request down rather than put in any effort to follow it up properly.

The structure of the organisation was set up to reflect the minimum manpower footprint that had existed a few weeks earlier, but with additional personnel posted in every week my first job was to reconfigure the EAW to reflect a more recognisable chain of command structure and this meant changing my job title to OC Engineering & Logistics (Eng & Logs). This restructuring was fairly easy to do, with each of the squadron leader posts taking responsibility for the areas that sat under their specialisation. Commanding Officer (CO) 906 EAW was a Tornado pilot and was a very decisive and forthright individual who was an outstanding CO. He made difficult decisions when required and had outstanding political skills when needed, and they were needed often. The base was home to a multitude of nations who all had their particular place in the pecking order and that usually boiled down to who had the biggest representation on the base or who had the most influence. The host nation (HN) obviously had the biggest say and they had a strange way of dealing with a lot of issues. The largest representation on the base other than the HN was the Australian Defence Force (ADF), followed by the UK and then very small contingents from the USA, the Netherlands and New Zealand.

The on-base and off-base rules of all the nationalities were also completely different and at times were bemusing. If you had been an alien looking down onto SLME you would have been scratching your head in disbelief trying to figure out exactly what was going on.

Nobody was allowed alcohol (understandable).

The HN was operating as normal as you would expect.

The ADF were living on base and were only allowed off base on rare occasions, and when they were allowed it was en masse by bus into the tourist areas and a bus back later in the day.

The UK were allowed off base on planned trips using contract hire cars but had to be back on base before midnight and had to travel with a minimum of two personnel in a vehicle.

The New Zealand and Netherlands personnel lived on base and were allowed to travel off base on planned trips in hire cars.

The USA personnel had been there the longest and had operated from the base for many years. As such they were living in rented accommodation in the centre of the city and travelling into work on a daily basis.

All of this was happening in a part of the world that had a massive tourist industry and an equally massive population of expats. It all seemed a bit bizarre but the regulations were there for a reason and pretty much to a man they were adhered to.

These regulations became ever more bizarre as the weeks and months went by with weird twists and turns on many occasions.

Throughout the duration of my tour, we had many high-profile, and not so high-profile, visitors coming out on visits to see how things were progressing and visiting was easy as there was a minimum of two military flights per week from the UK to SLME.

Some visitors used the military airbridge but for various reasons others chose to fly civilian into the local airport. If they flew civilian it meant that we had to send people to the airport to pick them up and vice versa on the return trip. On one such occasion we had an advance party from an Army unit who travelled out on civilian air, stayed in hotels and drove around the country in uniform, all of which was prohibited for the residents of SLME. The Army unit in question carried out at least three recces before they actually deployed on an exercise.

The aircrew and cabin crew on the twice weekly airbridge claimed that their crew rest time was always disturbed if they lived on base at SLME and as such always stayed in a hotel down town for their overnight stop. This necessitated busing the entire crew to the hotel and back again the following morning. It was a journey that could take up to an hour each way due to heavy traffic and was effectively taking away a few hours of their valuable rest time, especially as they had to change out of uniform before being taken off base and then change back into it when they returned the following morning. Plans were put in place to provide extra-quiet accommodation on base for the crews but they fought it for as long as they could and then once it was in place they complained about it endlessly. It all boiled down to change and the resistance to it but eventually the issues were overcome and living on base became the norm.

Much, if not all, of the life-support infrastructure on the base was provided by the ADF and once again this led to some strange rules being applied, particularly in the dining facility. Watching TV, you get the impression that the Australians have a similar culture to the UK but a bit more gung-ho and a bit more laid back.

Nothing could be further from the truth when it came to rules governing niff-naff and trivia. Most of the Brits using the dining facility would take off their combat dress shirts and dine in service-supplied

T-shirts but someone in the ADF took exception to this and we were told that we must dine in full combat uniform.

One day the RAF detachment warrant officer took me to one side and told me that the ADF had complained about our personnel attending the dining facility wearing thongs! Naturally I was horrified, as the thought of Brits walking around the base in tight and skimpy underwear was not what I expected on an operational tour and surely I would have noticed this alarming behaviour. The warrant officer could see the look of disbelief on my face and went on to explain that thongs were what the Australians called flip-flops. I was relieved that bare feet and not bare backsides was the only issue to be confronted. Everybody was rebriefed and complied with the latest request.

In parallel with a period of time during which the accommodation was becoming more occupied, PJHQ decided to let the contract hire of one of the accommodation complexes expire and instructed us to cram everybody into a single location. It was a good idea in principle but once again based on little knowledge of the real-time situation on the ground. We pleaded with them on several occasions to extend the contract for a few months until things stabilised and we had a better idea of the final number of personnel who would be permanently based at SLME. The contract expired, the accommodation plot started to fall apart and PJHQ asked us to try to negotiate an extension to the contract. As you would expect the contractor was well aware of our desperation and upped the price of the hire. PJHQ refused to pay the increased price and we had to resort to putting people three or four to a room, which was uncomfortable to say the least, especially when the air conditioning stopped working. Normally on this type of operational detachment, the accommodation starts off bad and gets better with time but due to PJHQ's inability to manage the situation this was the complete opposite. What started off fairly comfortably was now beginning to decline into overcrowding and squalor.

This job had the potential to be a fantastic opportunity and a great deal of fun at the same time. No two days were ever the same and every day brought a new and interesting challenge that had to be solved with little or no input from the UK hierarchy. Decisions needed to be made in an ever fluid and changing environment and the impact of all decisions was always felt immediately, whether it was good or bad. It was hugely refreshing to operate this way in an Air Force that had become cumbersome and unwieldy and it was like turning the clock back twenty years or more. We had to enjoy this way of operating while it lasted and make as much progress as possible before the inevitable over-regulation returned and the handbrake was applied with force.

The working conditions for many of the trades were not ideal as infrastructure was sparse and everybody had to make do with what they had or what they could beg, steal or borrow. The harshest conditions were experienced by the Trade Group (TG) 5 personnel who had two key roles to perform at SLME. One was to keep the ageing, overused and rapidly increasing number of specialist vehicles and ground support equipment running and the other was to continue the task of erection and maintenance of the temporary airfield infrastructure. There was no shelter in which to perform these tasks and the only way of mitigating against the intense heat was to carry out the work in the cooler hours of the day, but this was not always possible. What these individuals achieved in such arduous conditions against some brutal timelines was nothing short of outstanding. A party of 5001 Squadron Rapid Erect Shelter (RES) construction personnel was operating on the EAW when I arrived and this presented an ideal opportunity for me to see at first-hand what the squadron did as being their boss was going to be my next job. They too performed exceptionally well working in high temperatures to often ridiculously tight deadlines but without fail they delivered every time. The teams came back out several times during my time on the EAW to construct additional buildings and to maintain those that had been there for some time.

As part of my handover it was explained to me that a Royal Navy (RN) helicopter detachment were planning to deploy to SLME for a few months over the summer and that they had been promised some of the newly built infrastructure to operate from. I read through the email trail and saw that the majority of what had been promised was not available and was not even in the plan for the EAW. I sent an email to the RN and to PJHQ outlining what had been promised and what I thought was achievable within the timelines and this email highlighted a huge gap between the level of support expected and the reality of life on the ground. Despite the moaning from PJHQ, the RN were very pragmatic about the support we were offering and sent out a recce party to ascertain the reality of life at SLME. We agreed a level of support that was acceptable to all and when the advance party arrived, followed closely by the main party, what they achieved in a very short space of time was nothing short of remarkable. In a matter of days, they fully kitted out one of the large hangars that we had allocated to them with equipment and stores and were fully operational ahead of schedule.

To maintain a cool area in the hangar for ground crew recuperation I had made plans to have a domestic tent installed inside it that could be cooled with service-supplied air conditioning units to a much more comfortable temperature. To get this plan authorised I had to get approval from the fire service, who initially said it was impossible for me to do this as it contravened all fire regulations. After putting a case together and setting up a trial, it had to be sent back to Air Command for final approval and thankfully common sense prevailed and it was approved. The concept worked so well that we used it in various buildings for future visiting detachments.

As the pace of life started to settle down, the dreaded normalisation process started to kick in. Any request for new or additional equipment had to be put into a pre-formatted business case document and sent through the chain of command to PJHQ for approval, or more often than not rejection.

During aircraft exercises we were paying large amounts of money to hire in portable lighting equipment to illuminate the aircraft dispersal. I was aware that the RAF had lots of these lighting units spread all over the UK and decided to ask for some to be sent out to SLME as a long-term cost-saving measure. I was told that my idea would not be entertained unless I submitted my request on the official paperwork. I put forward my case based on the savings that would be made by not having to hire the lighting units from local firms. I was told that I had to be more specific as it was not clear why we needed the lights. I explained that personnel, vehicles and aircraft were operating from the dispersal and that the lights were needed for illumination of the area on safety grounds. I was told that it was still not clear why we needed the lights and as it was a new request it would be subject to intense scrutiny. By now I was at breaking point and wrote, 'It is not a new request as to the best of my knowledge it has always got dark at night in the ME.' The request was rejected so we carried on paying to hire lights and are probably still doing so today.

On another occasion, I was told by PJHQ that I had to submit a business case for an aircraft tow bar for one of our larger visiting aircraft. I was told that it was essential for us to have this piece of equipment and that I should submit the paperwork as soon as possible. I questioned the need and they explained to me that if the aircraft visited and needed to be moved I would need the tow bar. I pointed out that we did not have a tractor that was big enough to move the aircraft, so what was the point of having a tow bar and I went on to add that there were numerous types of aircraft that visited us for which we did not have tow bars. They could not see my point of view and went on to insist that I completed a business case and not to question their decision. I put the email trail and the request form in the 'to do' folder and it never raised its head again.

As part of the restructuring of the EAW, the CO decided that I was going to be his second in command (2i/c) and once again this was another huge boost for me and brought with it another level of responsibility that I was keen to fulfil. This 2i/c role also meant that when the CO went on R&R I took over the reins as CO 906 EAW. The CO flew out in the early hours at the start of his R&R and not long after start work on that day I was summoned to a meeting with the HN and went to get the keys for the CO's car to travel across base to the meeting. The keys were not there, so I called the movements office to see if the CO had left the keys with his car at movements when he flew out. They confirmed that both the car and keys were at movements but that they thought they would keep the car until the CO returned from his R&R. I pointed out that as the 2i/c I was now the acting CO and would need the vehicle to travel to meetings, as well as it being the car that was used by the EAW HQ staff officers when the CO was not using it. After much grumbling and gnashing of teeth the movements people returned the car to the HQ and I was able to travel to my meeting with the HN.

For a number of weeks, the HN runway lighting had been playing up and on several occasions it had failed completely, fortunately not at critical times. The ops people on 906 EAW had temporary runway lighting sent out to SLME and had been polishing them on a daily basis.

I asked if they had ever charged the lights up or turned them on to see if they worked and they had not so they began a schedule of charging and then carried out exercises to check that they were working and to practice what they would do if the lights were ever needed in earnest.

All seemed to be working well but they did not appear to work for very long until they ran out of charge. Shortly after CO 906 EAW went on R&R the runway lights started to fail on a more regular basis and the temporary lights were also showing signs of rapid deterioration. The situation came to a head about a week later when the runway lights failed and so did the temporary lights, leaving the airfield in total darkness. There was no exercise flying taking place but there were still quite a few operational flights that needed to continue. Some of the aircraft had crews who could operate in night vision goggles (NVG) but others did not and after consulting my fellow station execs we decided to close the airfield to UK aircraft. Dusk was falling and we were expecting a shuttle flight in the next couple of hours but only had sufficient runway lights to illuminate a percentage of the runway by using wider spacing between the lights. At the last moment we were told by ME HQ that the spacing of the lights was too much and therefore all flights must be diverted. The shuttle aircraft continued to approach the airfield and landed and I went to discuss with the aircrew the usefulness of the lighting as it did not meet the regulations and they stated that it was fine and that was why they continued with the landing. We spoke to ME HQ the following day and explained that the aircrew were reporting that the lighting was sufficient with the greater spacing but they flat out refused to authorise it. In the meantime, the HN had gone out and bought a brand-new set of temporary lighting (something they had been reluctant to do for the previous month or so) and the problem was remedied.

As the EAW was building up to its full capability we were still short of some vital personnel filling key roles. In particular, we did not have a Quality Assurance Co-ordinator (QAC), which for a fast-moving and dynamic engineering organisation was a massive gap.

All the other EAWs in the ME had a QAC, and in fact some had two. We completed all the relevant paperwork to have a post established but were told by some Army bloke in PJHQ that we did not need one. This was a strange statement from someone who, at best, had no idea what a

QAC was and was so inflexible that he did not even want to understand. The fact that every other RAF base in both the UK and in all deployed locations had a QAC except for us still didn't make him think or agree that something was fundamentally wrong.

The RAF engineering hierarchy in the ME and in the UK, whilst sympathetic to our cause, did very little to help the situation and stayed away from our location to make sure that they were not tarnished with what was going on at 906 EAW. Some idiot at HQ Air Command decided that it would be a good idea to carry out an External Quality Audit (EQA) on 906 EAW and planned for the team to visit in the middle of the summer.

EQAs are normally carried out on fully manned and well-established organisations and not fledgling organisations that are still finding their feet and coping with the day-to-day stresses of supporting multiple organisations operating from an austere location. Despite my protests it was decided that the EQA team would still carry out the audit as planned.

The EQA team arrived and my first job was to get them into the briefing room and give them a full overview of the EAW, warts and all. After my brief, they set about carrying out the audit and after a few days it was completed and they came to brief me and the CO on their findings.

Quality Occurrence Reports (QORs) is paperwork raised against specific failings in the system and they are designed to highlight failings in order to help to rectify them. The team had a list of potential QORs that they briefed us on and some of them were remarkable in that they had listened to my brief where I had identified areas of weakness and had turned my brief into a list of QORs. They had even raised a QOR against the EAW for us not having a QAC. As we had raised all of the necessary paperwork to establish the post but had been told by the ME and UK engineering hierarchy that there was nothing that could be done and had been told by PJHQ that we didn't need one, I suggested that the QOR should be raised against PJHQ. I was told that raising the QOR would help me get the post established. It did not and all it achieved was to make me carry out even more pointless staff work, duplicating what I had already done but still to no avail.

When the completed EQA report was sent to me a few weeks later the team had raised thirteen QORs against the EAW and all of them but two were outside of our control. We were working flat out on the EAW dealing with all sorts of issues and now I had to try to complete the EQA responses within thirty days. Again, this work would normally be carried out by the QAC, but of course we didn't have one. I was incensed that the organisation did not understand how hard we were working and how their lack of support was making it worse by the day. I worked through the night to produce a quick and dirty response to the EQA report and copied it to as many of the senior engineering managers in the RAF who had a stake in what we were doing at SLME. Within hours I had numerous responses, all stating how concerned they were with the report and wondering what could be done to improve the situation. I wrote back to them all explaining that none of the information was new and that none of it should have come as a surprise. I reiterated the numerous pleas for help that I had sent over the previous few months and expressed my dismay that it had taken this report to get everybody's attention.

Part of the EAW organisation was a small team known as the Tornado Maintenance Unit (TMU). Their job was to carry out routine and anti-deterioration maintenance on the Tornado aircraft that were stored there for use on exercises by the visiting squadrons. TMU was a very small team of personnel who more often than not had gaps in their skill levels due to the failure of manning to get people with the right qualifications and experience for the job.

Their shortfalls were highlighted during the EQA and as a result the Tornado Aircraft HQ from the UK decided to pay a visit to see how they could help. Whilst their support was much appreciated, when they arrived all they did was try to look after the Tornado-related side of the EAW and pay little interest to the rest of the problems. Their greatest achievement was to identify that TMU did not do maintenance as such and therefore they decided to change their name to the Tornado Anti-Deterioration Servicing Team. Priceless!

One day CO 906 EAW and I were summoned to the British Embassy to brief the Chief of the Defence Staff (CDS) on the work we were doing at SLME and how the infrastructure, international relations and the fast jet exercise programme were all developing. CO 906 EAW gave a very comprehensive brief on the progress being achieved at SLME in supporting operations in the Middle East and mentioned that during the fast jet exercises the aircrew were getting more experience of flying four-ship formations than at any time during their career. CDS's only question during the whole presentation was to ask why it was called a four-ship. Brilliant!

Whilst this job will go down as one of the best I have had in the RAF, it will also go down as the one that made me realise that, as my time in the service was coming to an end, it was probably time for me to go. During my six months in SLME I hosted aircraft exercises from three different aircraft squadrons of both Tornado and Typhoon. It was during these detachments that I met three senior engineering officers (SEngOs) who were obviously from a completely different planet to the one that I was from.

SEngO 1 saw little wrong when one of his aircraft taxied into a piece of ground equipment. Both aircrew members and the three-man see-off team thought that the aircraft was a bit close to an item of ground equipment (which was on wheels) but decided not to move it. As the aircraft wing passed over the ground equipment, one of the see-off team panicked and instructed the pilot to stop. As the brakes were applied, the aircraft dipped and the wing hit the ground equipment, puncturing the wing and putting the aircraft out of action for several days. The squadron carried out an investigation and the report apportioned no blame.

In my world; if five people think something on wheels should be moved I would move it rather than try to taxi the aircraft over it!

SEngO 2 travelled out with the largest advance party I had ever seen and once all the kit was unpacked the team waited for their aircraft to arrive. The SEngO met with me and CO 906 EAW to check the aircraft dispersal before the aircraft arrived and the SEngO commented that there was a lot of sand on the dispersal and he was not sure how that would affect the aircraft, or if indeed the aircraft would be able to use the area. Just to refresh your memory, we are at SLME in the middle of the desert and the SEngO is surprised that there is sand on the dispersal. We agreed to meet a few hours later to see if the situation had or could be improved. We met at the agreed time and the SEngO commented that things didn't look any better and that he was still very concerned.

The CO 906 EAW walked into one of the aircraft shelters, picked up a brush and started sweeping the dispersal. I looked at the SEngO and said, 'I think he is trying to make a point and don't expect him to sweep it all.' I asked what his massive advance party had been doing all day and he replied that they had been chilling out and getting ready for the aircraft to arrive. I pointed out that if he thought the area needed sweeping he could have got them to do it. I also highlighted again, just in case he hadn't realised, that we were in the middle of a desert and whatever was swept away now would be back in a couple of hours. He decided to 'risk it' and allowed the aircraft to land and taxi on to the dispersal. They did so and operated for a further five weeks without any sand-related issues.

SEngO 3 was also a little concerned about sand and insisted that we introduced a strict sweeping regime for the aircraft dispersal. We did so and agreed that we would use the road sweeper every other day or more often if needed. One of the tradesmen on his squadron decided that he would mark where the road sweeper was parked on a daily basis to catch us out if we did not use it as agreed. A few days later they were up in arms as the sweeper had not moved and they wanted to know why and who was going to be disciplined for not sweeping the dispersal. We pointed out that the sweeper was broken but the area had been swept using a HN sweeper and it was done before the squadron guys had even got out of bed. We took this opportunity to encourage the SEngO to get his guys to manually sweep the dispersal rather than play Tornado Inspector Clouseau if he was concerned.

In his spare time, and following on from his recce, SEngO 3 had produced a risk register, which he presented to me when he arrived with the advance party. When I first read through this register I started to smile as I thought it was a joke and when I started to laugh out loud the SEngO was taken aback by my attitude. I asked him if he was serious but I could tell instantly by the look on his face that he was. He had written a list of twenty entries and it was so bizarre and funny that I kept a copy to remind me why I was pleased that my time in the RAF was coming to an end. I will not itemise each and every entry but will just highlight the ones that in my mind were the most ridiculous:

Holes in the road between living accommodation and working accommodation. There was a risk that personnel could fall down the holes when transiting between areas.

Darkness and insufficient street lighting. There was a risk that personnel could fall over on the way to and from work due to insufficient street lighting.

Boredom. There was a danger that the ground crew could get very bored between aircraft sorties and shifts.

These were the most ridiculous ones but the others weren't that far away from being as crazy. I suggested that if he was that concerned he could got out and buy some torches and when the ground crew were bored he could get them to fill the holes in the road. He still did not see my point of view and instead went out and bought a TV and an Xbox from the Services Institute Funds for his guys to play on when they got bored.

Not long after this detachment arrived were told that we would be subjected to an explosive safety inspection by a small team from HQ Air Command. We highlighted to the team before they came out that we still had some problems that needed rectifying and pointed out the issues we had had with the EQA team. The team turned up as planned and initially started out in the same vein as the EQA team, being critical of what was going on at SLME and quoting rules and regulations to which we must adhere.

However, they very quickly realised that we were doing the best we could, given the situation, and they started to help us devise new plans and procedures that would help us to operate within regulations. Their pragmatic approach was well received by everybody on 906 EAW and in a short space of time we had made huge improvements.

Life on 906 EAW was extremely busy at all times, and even more so when fast jet detachments were operating. We were working long hours seven days a week but still managed to get a bit of free time, particularly when there were no aircraft exercising. We had regular games nights to help mould the unit together and started up what turned out to be a very competitive volleyball league. It was not only competitive within 906 EAW but we also had regular matches against the ADF. We formed an execs volleyball team and had a good group of players that was very competitive at all levels. There were those of us on the execs team that were ultra-competitive and those who were pleased just to play regardless of the result. As the execs were posted in and out we lost some very good players and had some 'not so good players' posted in. The competitive players, me included, were happy to play with a small nucleus of players that were of a good standard but sometimes the view was that if someone expressed an interest in taking part they should be able to. This was OK in friendly matches but we tried to avoid this situation if it was a league game.

During Ramadan the HN organised a series of sporting events in which all of the nationalities on the base were invited to take part. The events were wide ranging, from football to athletics to tug-of-war. The only snag with this event was that it had to take part in the evening because of Ramadan. By the time the HN participants had fasted for the day and then eaten to recover their energy and strength it meant that most events started at around 10 pm. Everybody took part and it was a good competition spread over a two-week period, throughout which every nation took a share of the wins and trophies.

Most of the personnel on the EAW had the opportunity to visit the local tourist hotspots as they were predominantly working on a shift system that allowed them some free time. The execs also had the opportunity during quiet moments and additionally we usually made the effort to go down town for something to eat if people were leaving. We visited a huge variety of eateries in town and had meals ranging from about £10 right up to £80 in some locations.

The whole of the EAW made significant efforts to improve living and working conditions, especially to the area inside the UK compound. We had several self-help projects to improve the quality of living and a great deal of time and effort was expended constructing sports and leisure areas, and we even constructed a beach area that could be used for sun bathing.

We had the use of the ADF coffee shop that was inside the ADF compound and we explored all the possibilities to try to get our own but although the indications were looking good when I left it had still not materialised. A senior officer payed a visit to our compound and his only comment was that our beach area made it look like a holiday camp and detailed us to either get rid of it or hide it. This was all a bit rich coming from an organisation that had a comfortable lifestyle, bars and regular trips to local hotels for relaxation.

Towards the end of my tour the infrastructure on the EAW became much in demand, particularly by visiting Army detachments. Additional living accommodation had been constructed and PJHQ were keen to get the use out of it when the opportunity arose. Again, from a living accommodation point of view this was not a huge problem but leisure facilities and dining facilities were still running at the same level, so once again life for the permanent staff became a little more uncomfortable. Most units turned up with all their kit but it was usually insufficient to operate fully and they were often dependent on the EAW for additional support, which was always given if we could facilitate.

With a few weeks of my tour to go I got an email from my replacement, who had just been nominated to replace me. I began the process of writing handover notes to make sure that nothing was forgotten or overlooked and as soon as he arrived I began the process of passing on all the information before preparing for my return to the UK.

With most of my handover complete I managed to cram in one more tourist trip into the city and then I was heading back to the UK via a quick stopover in Cyprus, as was routine for all returning flights. I arrived back at Brize Norton around lunchtime and was met by my wife, who had come to pick me up as the impasse between High Wycombe and Wittering as to whom I belonged had still not been resolved.

Chapter 22

RAF Wittering

After four weeks of much-needed leave it was time to arrive at RAF Wittering and start my new job as OC 5001 Squadron. It was only a few weeks before Christmas, so the station was on the rundown to a certain extent, which was good as it gave me the chance to ease myself into the job gradually.

This job was going to be a whole new experience as I had never worked closely with TG5 but a least my time in SLME had given me the opportunity to see them at work in the most arduous conditions and give me a good idea of what a varied world I was now going to be in charge of.

The overall organisation at Wittering hadn't changed since my tour on 5131 (BD) Squadron, so getting used to the station and wing hierarchy was relatively easy.

5001 Squadron were still recovering from the extensive work they had undertaken in SLME and people were taking the opportunity to use up some of their leave and extend the Christmas break. There were numerous rumours floating around about how busy we were going to be the following year and it was key that everybody took time to recharge their batteries, spend some quality time with their families and prepare for a very busy year.

During my arrival process, one of the other squadron leaders on the wing informed me that he had put my name forward to organise the upcoming royal visit by the Countess of Wessex. When I questioned why he had put my name forward, he told me that it was a good high-profile event and would help me get noticed! I reminded him that I had been in the RAF for thirty-seven years, was nearing the end of my career and that I had no need or desire to get noticed. He sheepishly apologised for his oversight, but to save him any trouble in identifying another individual to run the event I got one of the squadron flight commanders to organise and run the event with me providing oversight and top cover if needed.

The flight commander did an excellent job with very little input from me and the Royal visit was a resounding success.

After the Christmas and New Year break I started to get to grips with how the squadron was functioning and it was clear from the outset that it was very disjointed. This was primarily as a result of the way it had been originally formed by combining the two major TG5 elements on the unit under one banner. I met with the key personnel on the squadron, expressed my concerns and outlined my proposals for joining it all together. My proposals were met with resistance and resentment from the off and it was clear to me that restructuring the squadron into a seamless organisation was going to be an uphill battle. I decided that the best way to move my ideas forward was to concentrate on the small things first and chip away a piece at a time.

As the weeks rolled by the routine tasks started to build up but problems with the provision of spares for some of the ageing temporary shelters around the military was proving to be a problem. I put a proposal to the support authority to remove our commitment to maintaining these structures based on lack of spares, lack of documentation and a potential ground rush of new tasks coming up throughout the year. It took a while and a lot of convincing but soon we would be free of this onerous task, leaving us to concentrate on the more important operational tasking.

A fast jet deployment to the Baltic region for NATO air policing duties was the first major task on the list and following on from a recce the squadron was tasked with constructing four new shelters at an airbase in the Baltics.

Soon after that task came in and a team were dispatched there was talk of the draw down of operations in Afghanistan and planning had started in earnest for closing the UK mission at Kandahar airfield.

All the temporary aircraft shelters that had previously been erected by 5001 Squadron had been handed over to a civilian contractor but it now seemed that they were unable to meet the tight schedule for the draw down and recovery of equipment. The schedule was very tight and had been combined with the reduction of aircraft and troop numbers, and as such the plan could not be allowed to slip. Therefore, it was decided that 5001 Squadron would put a huge team together to deploy to Kandahar to assist with the draw down operation.

When they said 'assist with' what they really meant was 'carry out the lion's share of' the dismantling task. This was going to be the biggest ever deployment of 5001 Squadron personnel in modern times and as such we decided to send a small management team consisting of the flight commander and one of the flight sergeants to provide top cover for the teams and to make sure that they were not railroaded into any additional tasking that would divert them from their primary task.

The team deployed in phases to coincide with the draw down and soon after all the personnel were in theatre the additional tasks started to feed into the squadron HQ back at Wittering. The more routine ones could be deferred but several high-priority tasks came up that we had not been expecting as well as some routine operational jobs that could not be put off. The first request was to have one of the Kandahar shelters re-erected at Kabul and that was quickly followed by requests to have the routine maintenance and repairs of shelters in the Baltics and SLME carried out.

But more pressing, due to the developing situation with Islamic State in Iraq and Syria, was a request to construct shelters at RAF Akrotiri in Cyprus for use by the fast jet aircraft that would be deploying there to support the operation.

With all available personnel already in Afghanistan we started to look at how the Kandahar task was progressing and how we could divert personnel to the other task when needed. It was going to take time to get the shelters to Cyprus, so we had a few weeks to play with and started planning how and when we were going to move the teams.

The task at Kandahar was going well and they were slightly ahead of schedule, so we redeployed part of the management team to Cyprus to carry out a recce to make sure that everything was in place for the new shelters and to plan and agree a location for them. The first team to complete their allotted task at Kandahar was redeployed to Kabul to carry out a recce there and some personnel were sent back to SLME to carry out repairs and maintenance. The team that carried out the recce to Kabul were brought back to the UK to get some additional training and downtime before flying back out to start erecting the shelter as soon as it arrived. Within a couple of months all the teams had deployed to Afghanistan, completed the deconstruction task, returned to the UK and then redeployed to Afghanistan, Cyprus, the Baltics and SLME.

This was a further extension of an extremely busy period throughout which most of the Operations Flight team had deployed, leaving very few personnel back at base. Everybody made it back in time for Christmas, which was my initial wish, but for the team at Kandahar it was very close and they only made it with a couple of days to spare.

Whilst all of this work had been going on overseas, I was still chipping way in the background at trying to make the squadron a more joined up organisation. We were getting there slowly with combined training teams and standardised practices between the flights, and whilst we were still some way off my ideal solution we were certainly making progress. Several of the middle management team on the squadron had changed over in a short space of time and this again lent itself to making changes that had previously been resisted by some.

One of my more satisfying roles as the squadron boss was to maintain the historic links between the squadron and the members of the Airfield Construction Officers' Association (ACOA) and the Airfield Construction Branch (ACB). Not long after arriving on the squadron I got a call from the Secretary of the ACOA inviting me out for a pub lunch and a chat. I arrived at the pub in good time and was greeted by the ACOA Secretary who, after a short introduction, got straight to the point and asked me to speak at an upcoming ACOA social function. As I pointed out at the time, I was aware there was no such thing as a free lunch and agreed to attend the function and speak about what the squadron had been up to. Later that year I attended the ACOA annual dinner in the RAF Club in London with my wife, paid for my free lunch and had a fantastic evening with all the ACOA members.

Later in the year I got a call from the ACB asking for my help. A memorial had been dedicated to those members of the airfield construction organisation who had been killed in a bombing raid at Great Chart near Ashworth in Kent during the Second World War and they were struggling to get any representation from Air Command to attend the ceremony.

Other nationalities were providing some fairly senior representation and the ACB wanted the RAF representation to be at a similar level. I agreed to attend the ceremony and was very pleased to have done so. After spending the day with numerous members of the ACB and their families I was honoured to lay a wreath in their name to the members of the organisation who had been killed on that fateful day. The whole event had been planned by the local villagers and had been years in the making.

Such was the commitment and dedication of the locals that one of the local families made their house available for me to get changed into my number one uniform for the event. The whole thing had been planned to perfection with a grandstand erected, a very emotional and moving DVD film playing in the church before the service, and an afternoon tea in the village hall with history archives and storyboards adorning the hall. It all culminated in a sunset ceremony and wreath laying at the newly commissioned memorials. Following on from this event the ACB asked me to attend their annual dinner in Chester and once again I agreed to go along and sing for my supper. It was a great opportunity to practice my speech for the ACOA dinner later in the year; the ACB could not have been more welcoming and were superb hosts for the evening.

It was during my time on 5001 Squadron that one of the EOD operators who was on 5131 (BD) Squadron when I was the OC sent an email out looking for anybody that might be interested in buying a specially commissioned BD watch to commemorate the seventy-fifth anniversary of RAF EOD. The minimum order for the one-off commission was fifty. As there were over 100 people on 5131 (BD) Squadron and thirty working in other organisations, plus in the height of the Cold War there were thirty-plus personnel on each of the large RAF units there should have been no trouble in achieving the total. Oh, how wrong I was! Very few people were interested and, in the end, he had to go back to the manufacturers and see if a commission could be secured for a smaller amount. With a small increase in price the manufacturer agreed to go ahead with the project for a guaranteed order of thirty-five. Believe it or not even getting that number was a struggle but was eventually achieved. The personalised, engraved order was completed and those who received watches were extremely happy with the final product. During my first tour of duty on 5131 (BD) Squadron we had a memorabilia shop where we all bought squadron-specific, T-shirts, badges, tie pins, Zippo lighters and even model cars. Sadly, the pride that most people felt while serving on 5131 (BD) Squadron was not a lasting one and perhaps is just a sign of the times.

After only fifteen months in the job it was time to start planning for my departure as my exit date was drawing ever closer. Once I had worked out how much annual and terminal leave and resettlement time I had coming to me it was obvious that my time in the RAF was very quickly coming to the end and it was time to hand over the reins of the squadron to one of the flight commanders and start making my final exit plan.

Just as I had planned and organised my last few months and worked out what I had to do before I left the RAF, the wing commander called me and asked me how I felt about heading up a team of people to go out to RAF Akrotiri in Cyprus to try and get to the bottom of some key issues they had been having on the base in supporting the current operations with TG5 manpower.

I said I was more than happy to go as it looked like an important and interesting job, had the potential to help make a real difference and also gave me the opportunity for a swansong in the sun.

We arrived in Cyprus and quickly set about looking at the specified areas and it became evident very quickly that the problems were deep rooted in the fact that Akrotiri was still operating in its own unique way to its own unique hours regardless of the fact that there were twenty-four-hour operations being carried out by the fast jet squadrons. There was a shortage of manpower in some key critical areas but despite 5001 Squadron sending people to assist nothing had been done about identifying and putting in place a permanent solution. After a week of carrying out interviews, visits and analysis we returned to the UK and compiled a report to be sent to HQ Air Command that identified the issues and suggested some quick fix solutions to the problems.

A week or so later the wing commander called me to his office and thanked me for my work. He said that Air Command had transferred my report into a spreadsheet that identified the issues in the traffic light system of red, amber and green identifiers. He could see the blood draining from my face and asked what was wrong.

I told him that in my view anything transferred to the traffic light spreadsheet was seen as done by the HQ and that I was now confident that nothing would get done to resolve the issues.

Example: We can't do this! Transfer to spreadsheet as red.

There it is fixed now because we have identified that we can't do it.

Problem solved.

Further confirmation to me, if I needed any, that it was time to go.

I said my goodbyes to everyone, handed in my uniform and went home to enjoy my retirement. I came back after about a month for my final leaving function, which had been organised by OC Operations Flight on 5001 Squadron.

It was a fantastic occasion attended by people who I had worked with right throughout my career. There were work colleagues there from every stage of my career from basic training right through all of my postings to my final job as OC 5001 Squadron. It was great to see them all, members of my family joined us in the bar after the dinner and it was a fitting end to my fantastic career.

I have loved every minute of my time in the RAF, I have had good jobs and great jobs peppered with a few forgettable ones but in the main it has been fantastic. Given the chance I would do it all again with maybe just a few minor tweaks here and there. I look back now and think how fortunate I have been to have done a job that I loved and travelled all over the world in doing it.

Epilogue

Despite my best efforts during my time at HQ Air Command to convince the hierarchy that RAF bomb disposal was a capability worth keeping, regrettably my hard work and commitment had only given it a stay of execution.

At the time of my book being taken on by the publishers it was announced by the RAF that it would start winding down its bomb disposal capability, 5131 (BD) Squadron, with a view to it disappearing completely from the RAF inventory by April 2020.

It is with great sadness that more than seventy-five years of history, blood, sweat and tears is to come to an end at the stroke of a pen for what are undoubtedly budget constraints. The pride and passion of all of those who have served on RAF bomb disposal and particularly 5131 (BD) Squadron will never be forgotten by those select few personnel who had the honour to serve with them and those who served alongside them.

The RAF bomb disposal capability was established in 1939 at the onset of the Second World War and it had its first task when a bomb was dropped on RAF Sullom Voe in the Shetland Islands. In May 1940 the first German bomb to be dropped on mainland Britain fell near Canterbury in Kent.

From those early days during the Second World War when the capability was established to dispose of the thousands of bombs dropped by the Luftwaffe through to the more recent operational tours, many of which are featured in this book, the RAF bomb disposal personnel have battled constantly with the lack of interest from the RAF hierarchy, unless, of course, there is an immediate requirement and then they become flavour of the month. This sporadic lethargy has been accompanied by the constant threats of takeover and sniping from the Army.

- During the Second World War the RAF bomb disposal organisation employed more than 1,000 personnel in full-time bomb disposal duties. After the war, RAF bomb disposal formed part of the Allied Disarmament Organisation across Europe and between 1945 and 1947 they dealt with more than 161,000 tonnes of conventional ordnance, more than 28,000 tonnes of chemical weapons and 4,370 'V' weapons.

- During the Falklands conflict RAF bomb disposal personnel were deployed but only in small numbers. They had a successful operation and the team leader was awarded the Queens Gallantry Medal (QGM) for sleeping with an unexploded bomb until sunrise when it could be dealt with. He did so to keep up the spirits of the injured personnel who could not be moved from the field hospital at Ajax Bay. RAF bomb disposal teams have been deployed to the Falkland Islands ever since and are still there today.

- RAF Bomb Disposal teams were some of the first to cross the border from Kuwait to Iraq during Operation Granby in 1991.

- During the Cold War every RAF Germany unit and many of the UK units had twelve bomb disposal teams on standby to clear the airfield if the unimaginable ever happened. The vast majority of those personnel were armament tradesmen and women first and bomb disposal operators second who had to carry out regular additional training to ensure their skills were maintained at a very high standard.

- During Operation Agricola, four bomb disposal teams and a commander were some of the first military personnel to undertake the initial entry into Kosovo. One team remained in the country on a six-month rotation for many years.

- In 2003, around fifty RAF bomb disposal personnel were deployed to five countries (Kuwait, Saudi Arabia, Qatar, Jordan and Cyprus) in support of Operation Telic in Iraq. Once the initial entry into Iraq had been completed the number of teams was drawn down but the RAF maintained a permanent presence on the operation until it finished in 2010.

- A small contingent from 5131(Bomb Disposal) Squadron was sent to Afghanistan in 2001 to clear the airfield at Kabul and returned after five months once the task was complete. However, the squadron was to return to Afghanistan in 2010 as part of the Joint EOD organisation on Operation Herrick. Many of the flight commanders on the squadron completed operational tours, as did many personnel in different roles. They ranged from IED destroy teams right through to high-threat IEDD teams. Some worked in RAF teams, some in mixed RAF and Army teams and some of the junior ranks were so keen to get involved they even volunteered to work as EOD assistants on Army teams.

- The squadron currently has personnel deployed on Operation Shader in support of operations over Iraq and Syria to defeat ISIS.

- Up until April 2019, 5131(Bomb Disposal) Squadron had two teams permanently on immediate standby 24/7 for MACP assistance. Over the years they have carried out an average of ninety-seven tasks per year, both IEDD and CMD. In addition to all of the above they have been constantly providing teams to carry out the clearance of UK air weapon ranges and providing support to weapon trials, tests and development.

- As well as having RAF bomb disposal personnel in the front-line operational roles, the RAF also has key personnel in the MoD, joint service training organisations and numerous support and staff roles. They have also provided operational and training personnel to support the Army in Northern Ireland and on overseas training teams.

- The formation of the RAF EOD EDIT (formerly the EOD Development Team) meant that no longer did we have to wait for weapons to go wrong before we worked out how to deal with them and make them safe. We were involved with industry during the design and manufacture of the weapons and had an in-depth knowledge of how they were made up and how they worked.

Throughout its long and proud history, the personnel of the RAF EOD organisation have been awarded numerous honours and awards as detailed in the table below:

Rank & Name	Award	Year	Rank & Name	Award	Year
WO Charlton	GC	1940	Flt Lt Rutter	MBE	1946
Flt Lt Dowland	GC		Flt Lt Marshal	MBE	
Mr Harrison	GC		Flt Lt Waters	MBE	
Sqn Ldr Moxey	GC		Flt Lt Tottey	MBE	
WO Hunt	GM		Flt Lt Durrant	MBE	
Wg Cdr Stevens	OBE	1941	FS Clarke	BEM	1958
FS Handford	BEM		Sgt Mulholland	BEM	
WO Alford	GM	1942	Cpl Hooper	BEM	1978
WO Saunders	GM		Flt Lt Swan	QGM	1982
Sgt Lythgoe	GM		Jnr Tech Thorne	QCB	
AC2 Nicholson	GM		SAC Soppet-Moss	QCB	
AC2 Simpson	GM		FS Knights	MiD	
WO Bishop	GM		Wg Cdr Symonds	OBE	1988
Flt Lt Dickinson	GM		Sqn Ldr Swan	MBE	1989
Sqn Ldr Rowlands	MBE		FS Waldock	BEM	1990
Wg Cdr Rowlands MBE	GC	1943	Flt Lt Shears	MBE	1990
WO Stevens	GM	1944	Sgt Rogers	GM	1992
Sqn Ldr Clark	OBE	1946	FS Shaw	MBE	1993
Sqn Ldr Dinwoodie OBE MC	GC		Sgt Roberts	MBE	1993
Cpl Garred BEM	GM		Chief Tech Barlow	QCB	2003
AC1 Halton	BEM		Chief Tech Barlow	MBE	2003
Sqn Ldr Reed	MBE		Chief Tech Pounder	MiD	2003
Flt Lt Rulf	MBE		Chief Tech Lowe	QGM	2011

* all details taken from operational honours board located at RAF Wittering.

To all of those personnel who worked in RAF bomb disposal, in whatever guise: you should be immensely proud of what you achieved in difficult circumstances doing a job that was generally thankless and ultimately dangerous.

Hopefully the RAF will not find out the hard way that: 'You don't know what you've got till it's gone'

E Nocentibus Innocentia

Index